T0039092

Cyber Guardians

Cyber Guardians

*Empowering Board
Members for Effective
Cybersecurity*

Bart R. McDonough

WILEY

May you forever rest in peace, my sweet Momma.

To my thoughtful, kind, introspective, hardworking, and joyful son, Russell Eric McDonough.
Keep being you.

Contents

Contents

Contents

Preface: What to Expect from This Book

As a board member, you may not have extensive knowledge of cybersecurity, but you are responsible for ensuring that your organization has effective cybersecurity measures in place. This book aims to provide practical guidance to help you fulfill this responsibility.

In the following chapters, we will cover various cybersecurity topics in depth, such as threat actors, data breaches, compliance regulations, risk assessments, and incident response. But more importantly, we will provide you with the tools to translate this information into actionable steps that you can take to protect your organization.

Throughout the book, you can expect to find real-world examples, case studies, and best practices that will help you understand the material in a practical context. We have purposely made the content accessible and easy to understand, focusing on practical application over technical jargon.

In addition to the theoretical concepts, we also include several checklists, templates, and questions that you can use to evaluate your organization's current cybersecurity posture and be sure you are asking the right questions of the right people. We want to give you the tools to ensure your organization's strong cybersecurity culture.

Finally, we will emphasize the importance of collaboration and communication between the board, the C-suite, and the cybersecurity team. While this book is focused on board members, it is useful for executives and cybersecurity professionals as well. By working together, we can build a cybersecurity culture that will protect our organizations and benefit our customers, employees, and shareholders.

This book aims to be a practical guide for board members who want to take an active role in their organization's cybersecurity posture. We will provide you with the information and tools you need to translate cybersecurity concepts into practical steps that you can take to protect your organization.

Chapter 1
Introduction

The digital age has significantly expanded the responsibilities of a board member in a small or medium-sized business (SMB), pushing the boundaries beyond conventional business oversight. A key element of this new, expanded role is safeguarding the company from an array of risks. Among these, cyber threats stand out due to their potentially devastating consequences, which could include reputational damage, substantial financial losses, and legal liabilities.

In today's interconnected world, cybersecurity is a matter of paramount importance for businesses of all sizes. With the escalation in complexity and sophistication of cyber threats, board members are now obliged to arm themselves with the knowledge and tools required to protect their organizations from such malicious attacks.

Over the years, the landscape of cyber threats has undergone significant transformations. Cyberattacks have become increasingly sophisticated and frequent, causing cybersecurity governance to emerge as a crucial consideration for SMBs. A single cyber breach can have profound consequences, including compromising sensitive company data, tarnishing the company's reputation, and, in the worst cases, leading to the business's dissolution.

This book aims to assist board members of SMBs in understanding the pivotal role of cybersecurity governance in the contemporary business landscape. It offers a comprehensive guide to the multifaceted world of cybersecurity governance, illuminating key concepts and terminology, prevalent cyber threats and associated risks, legal and regulatory factors, and best practices for managing and mitigating these risks.

The book seeks to inform board members about their role in overseeing cybersecurity, elucidate the process of creating an effective cybersecurity governance framework, and propose methods for identifying, assessing, and prioritizing cyber risks. Moreover, it delves into the development and implementation of a comprehensive cybersecurity program, managing third-party risk, fostering cybersecurity training and awareness, and considering the role of cyber insurance.

An essential aspect of cybersecurity governance involves understanding the cyber threat landscape, including the various types of cyber threats and threat actors that organizations face today. The book will explore the legal and regulatory requirements governing cybersecurity, such as the Federal Trade Commission (FTC) Act, California Consumer Privacy Act (CCPA), General Data Protection Regulation (GDPR), Payment Card Industry Data Security Standard (PCI DSS), Sarbanes-Oxley Act (SOX), and Department of Financial Services (DFS) cybersecurity regulations. Each case is discussed in detail, shedding light on violations and the extent of board members' involvement in these incidents.

Equally crucial is understanding the importance of risk management and assessments. This book covers various forms of assessments like penetration testing, vulnerability scanning, security risk assessments, threat modeling, social engineering assessments, and compliance assessments. It will provide board members with the critical insights required when presenting the results of these assessments. The book underlines the need for a proactive approach to cybersecurity, emphasizing the importance of fostering a cybersecurity culture within organizations. It highlights practical guidance on establishing a tailored cybersecurity program to address the unique needs of an organization.

Furthermore, the book incorporates real-world case studies and examples of cybersecurity incidents, including those that violated data breach notification laws and instances where boards of directors were involved. Learning from these incidents and understanding the lessons gleaned from them can better equip board members to safeguard their organizations against future cyberattacks.

The evolving nature of cyber threats makes them an inevitability rather than a possibility. A single breach can wreak irreparable damage on a company, making appropriate management of cybersecurity risks crucial. However, with comprehensive cybersecurity governance, SMBs can mitigate these risks and protect their businesses.

This book serves as an invaluable resource for board members of SMBs, deepening their understanding of cybersecurity governance's importance and guiding them in taking the necessary protective measures. By implementing effective cybersecurity strategies, SMBs can reduce their exposure to cyber threats and boost their resilience to potential cyberattacks.

Throughout this book, board members will be equipped with the knowledge and tools needed to navigate the intricate world of cybersecurity. The goal is to ensure the safety and success of businesses in the digital age by transforming cybersecurity from a daunting challenge into an empowering part of their corporate governance strategy.

Cybersecurity Incident: Yahoo

One of the most notorious examples of how a cyber-security breach can damage a company's reputation, value, and future prospects is the case of Yahoo. In 2013, the Internet giant suffered a massive cyberattack that compromised the personal data of all its 3 billion user accounts, including names, email addresses, passwords, phone numbers, and security questions. The hackers behind the attack were later identified as state-sponsored actors from Russia.

However, Yahoo's board of directors did not act swiftly or transparently to address the breach and its implications. Instead of notifying the company's users and the public immediately, the board waited until 2016 to disclose the breach, after another separate breach that affected 500 million accounts was revealed. The board also failed to conduct a thorough investigation of the breach and its root causes and did not implement adequate cybersecurity measures to prevent future attacks.

The board's negligence and delay had serious consequences for Yahoo and its stakeholders. The breach and the disclosure eroded the trust and confidence of Yahoo's users, advertisers, partners, and regulators. The breach also affected Yahoo's valuation and deal negotiations with Verizon, which agreed to buy Yahoo's core Internet business in 2016. After learning about the breach, Verizon lowered its offer by $350 million and required Yahoo to share the legal liabilities arising from the breach. The deal was finalized in 2017, with Yahoo selling its Internet assets for $4.48 billion, a fraction of its peak value of over $100 billion in 2000.

(continued)

(continued)

Yahoo's board also faced legal repercussions for its mishandling of the breach. The board was sued by several shareholders who accused it of breaching its fiduciary duty and failing to protect the company's assets. The board also faced an investigation by the Securities and Exchange Commission (SEC), which charged it with violating federal securities laws by misleading investors about the breach. In 2018, the board agreed to settle the shareholder lawsuit for $80 million and pay a $29 million fine to the SEC, marking the first time that a public company was penalized by the SEC for a cybersecurity disclosure failure.

Yahoo's case illustrates how a cybersecurity breach can have devastating effects on a company's performance, reputation, and survival. It also shows how board members have a critical role and responsibility to oversee their company's cybersecurity strategy, governance, and risk management. Board members need to be aware of the cyber threats facing their company, ask the right questions of their management and IT security teams, ensure timely and accurate disclosure of any breaches, and take proactive steps to enhance their company's cyber resilience. By doing so, board members can protect their company's interests and fulfill their fiduciary duty to their shareholders and stakeholders.

Summary of a Board's Incident Response

When a company has a cybersecurity incident, the board of directors needs to be informed as soon as possible. Once informed, the board's first priority is to understand the nature and scope of the incident, including the potential impact on the company, its customers, and other stakeholders.

The board should also ensure that the company has an effective incident response plan in place and that the plan is being followed. The incident response plan should include steps for containing the incident, investigating the cause, and mitigating the damage. The plan should also specify the roles and responsibilities of the different members of the incident response team and outline the communication and reporting procedures.

Additionally, the board should work with management to assess the incident's potential legal and regulatory implications, including the company's obligations to report the incident to law enforcement and regulatory agencies. The board should also ensure that the company is taking appropriate steps to notify customers and other affected parties and provide them with information and support.

Finally, the board should conduct a post-incident review to identify the root cause of the incident and assess the effectiveness of the company's response. This review should include an analysis of the company's cybersecurity posture and risk management processes and should identify any areas for improvement. The board should use the review findings to update the incident response plan and ensure that the company is better prepared to prevent and respond to future incidents.

Cybersecurity Incident: Equifax

Equifax, one of the largest credit reporting agencies in the United States, faced a major crisis in 2017 when it disclosed that a data breach had exposed the

(continued)

sensitive information of more than 143 million consumers, including names, Social Security numbers, birth dates, addresses, and driver's license numbers. The breach also affected some customers in Canada and the UK. The hackers who perpetrated the breach exploited a known vulnerability in a web application that Equifax had failed to patch in time.

The board of directors of Equifax came under fire for its inadequate response and accountability for the breach. The board was accused of being unaware of the company's cybersecurity risks and capabilities and failing to provide sufficient oversight and guidance to the management and IT security teams. The board was also criticized for not disclosing the breach to the public and regulators for six weeks after discovering it and for allowing some senior executives to sell their shares before the disclosure. The breach resulted in the resignation of the company's CEO, CIO, and CSO, as well as several board members, including the board's chairman.

The board formed a special committee to conduct an independent review of the breach and its causes. The committee's report, released in 2018, revealed that the board had not received adequate information or training on cybersecurity matters and had not clearly defined its role and responsibilities in overseeing the company's cybersecurity. The report also found that the company had not implemented proper security policies and procedures and had not followed best practices for incident response and disclosure. The report made several recommendations for improving the board's cybersecurity governance, such as establishing a technology

(continued)

(continued)
committee, enhancing cybersecurity reporting and metrics, providing regular cybersecurity education and awareness sessions, and hiring external experts to assess and monitor the company's cybersecurity posture.

The breach had severe consequences for Equifax and its stakeholders. The company faced multiple lawsuits from consumers, investors, customers, and regulators, as well as congressional hearings and investigations. The company agreed to pay up to $700 million in settlements and fines to various parties, including the FTC, Consumer Financial Protection Bureau (CFPB), state attorneys general, and consumer groups. The company also suffered reputational damage and lost business opportunities due to the breach.

The incident underscored the importance of board involvement and leadership in cybersecurity governance. Board members need to be informed about and engaged in their company's cybersecurity strategy, risk assessment, and incident response. Board members also need to ensure that their company has adequate resources, processes, and controls to protect its data and assets from cyber threats. By doing so, board members can safeguard their company's reputation, value, and trust.

Checklist for a Board's Incident Response

Here is a checklist for what a board of directors should address when their company has a major cybersecurity incident:

1. *Notify appropriate personnel.* Ensure that the incident response team is immediately notified and a plan of action is implemented.
2. *Assess the situation.* Determine the extent of the breach and the potential impact on the organization's assets, reputation, and stakeholders.
3. *Determine the cause.* Identify the incident's root cause and the vulnerability that was exploited.
4. *Contain the damage.* Isolate the affected systems, and limit further damage.
5. *Collect evidence.* Preserve any evidence related to the incident, and ensure that it is properly documented.
6. *Notify stakeholders.* Inform all relevant stakeholders about the incident, and provide regular updates on the status of the investigation.
7. *Involve legal and regulatory authorities.* Consult with legal and regulatory authorities and external cybersecurity experts to ensure that all requirements are met.
8. *Review and update policies and procedures.* Review and update the organization's cybersecurity policies and procedures to prevent future incidents.
9. *Communicate with the board.* As often a few board members will focus on the incident, it is important to keep the entire board informed of the incident and provide regular updates on the investigation's progress and steps to mitigate the impact.
10. *Conduct a post-incident review.* Conduct a comprehensive review of the incident to identify areas for improvement and update policies and procedures as necessary.

The following chapters delve into all these consideration.

Chapter 2
Cybersecurity Basics

In the rapidly evolving digital landscape, understanding the basics of cybersecurity is no longer a luxury but a necessity, particularly for board members tasked with overseeing their organization's cybersecurity posture. This chapter provides a comprehensive exploration of the fundamental concepts and principles that underpin cybersecurity, serving as a foundation for the more advanced topics discussed in later chapters.

We begin by introducing the confidentiality, integrity, and availability (CIA) framework, a cornerstone of cybersecurity that outlines the three main objectives of any robust security strategy. Understanding this framework is crucial for board members as it provides a lens through which to view and evaluate the effectiveness of their organization's cybersecurity measures.

Next, we delve into key cybersecurity concepts and terminology that board members need to know. This includes an overview of common cyber threats and risks faced by companies today. From malware and phishing attacks to insider threats and data breaches, understanding these threats is the first step in building a resilient cybersecurity strategy.

As the cyber landscape is continually evolving, we also discuss emerging threats that companies need to be aware of. This includes an exploration of the latest technologies and defense strategies that can be employed to mitigate these threats. Understanding these technologies and strategies is vital for board members to make informed decisions about their organization's cybersecurity investments.

Threat intelligence, another critical aspect of cybersecurity, is also covered in this chapter. We discuss how threat intelligence can provide actionable insights about the current threat landscape, enabling companies to proactively defend against potential cyberattacks.

We then delve into the various threat actors in the cyber landscape, from individual hackers to state-sponsored groups, and their motivations. Understanding the capabilities and tactics of these threat actors can help board members assess the level of risk their organization faces.

Finally, we introduce the MITRE ATT&CK framework, a globally accessible knowledge base of adversary tactics and techniques. This framework can be a valuable tool for board members to understand the various tactics, techniques, and procedures (TTPs) that threat actors use, enabling them to better evaluate their organization's defenses.

This chapter provides a comprehensive overview of the fundamental concepts and principles of cybersecurity. By understanding these basics, board members can play a more active and effective role in their organization's cybersecurity governance, helping to protect their organization from the ever-present threat of cyberattacks.

Cybersecurity Incident: JBS

JBS, one of the world's largest meat suppliers, suffered a ransomware attack in May 2021. The company's board of directors and management team were forced to temporarily halt operations at several processing plants in the United States, Canada, and Australia due to the attack, which resulted in the company's IT systems shutting down. JBS later paid the hackers an $11 million ransom to restore its operations. The incident highlighted the growing threat of ransomware attacks against critical infrastructure, including the food supply chain, and the need for robust cybersecurity measures to protect against such attacks.

CIA Framework

The CIA framework is a fundamental concept in cybersecurity that board members should understand. This framework defines the goals of cybersecurity in terms of three key areas.

- *Confidentiality* is defined as ensuring that data and information are not disclosed to unauthorized parties.

  It refers to the protection of sensitive information from unauthorized access or disclosure. For example, a board member may have access to sensitive financial information or strategic plans for the company. It is important that this information is kept confidential to prevent competitors or malicious actors from accessing it.

Measures that can be taken to ensure confidentiality include implementing access controls, such as passwords and two-factor authentication, to limit access to sensitive information to only authorized individuals. Encryption can also be used to protect data from being read by unauthorized individuals, even if they are able to access the data.

Maintaining confidentiality is crucial in protecting the company's sensitive information and ensuring that it remains secure.

- *Integrity* is defined as maintaining the accuracy and completeness of data and information.

In other words, data cannot be modified or altered by unauthorized persons or means. Data integrity ensures that the data remains consistent and accurate throughout its life cycle and is protected from unauthorized modification.

Examples of data integrity breaches include unauthorized changes to files or documents, such as altering or deleting data, as well as system or application tampering that may cause critical data to become corrupted or lost. For instance, if a hacker were to gain access to a company's financial system and alter the data to create fake transactions, the breach could result in significant financial losses for the company.

Ensuring data integrity requires implementing appropriate security measures, such as access controls, encryption, and audit logs. Encryption protects the confidentiality and integrity of data by preventing unauthorized parties from accessing or modifying it, while audit logs track and record all system activities to help detect and prevent unauthorized changes to data.

Board members should be aware of the importance of data integrity and ensure that their organization's cybersecurity strategy includes measures to protect it.

This may involve implementing security controls, such as access controls and audit logs, as well as conducting regular vulnerability assessments and penetration testing to identify and address potential vulnerabilities in the system.

- *Availability* is defined as ensuring that data and information are accessible to authorized parties when needed. This means the information and systems are up and running and there is no disruption to business operations.

For example, if a company's website is the main way customers purchase products, it is critical that the website is always available. Any downtime or disruption could result in lost sales and damage to the company's reputation. A company may also rely on other systems, such as email or file sharing, to conduct business. Business operations may be delayed or employee productivity may be impacted if these systems are unavailable.

To ensure availability, companies may implement measures, such as redundancy and backup systems, disaster recovery plans, and monitoring tools to detect and quickly respond to any disruptions. This includes ensuring that hardware, software, and network infrastructure are regularly maintained, updated, and tested to prevent outages.

In summary, availability is an essential aspect of the CIA framework, and it is crucial for board members to understand the importance of ensuring that systems and information are always accessible to authorized users.

To effectively manage cybersecurity risks, it is important to consider all three aspects of the CIA framework. While a company may prioritize confidentiality by encrypting sensitive data, if that data becomes unavailable when needed, it could have a negative impact on the business. Similarly, maintaining data integrity is important to ensure that decisions are based on accurate and complete information.

Board members should understand the CIA framework and how it can be applied to their company's cybersecurity program. By prioritizing the confidentiality, integrity, and availability of data and information, the company can better manage cybersecurity risks and protect against cyber threats. Additionally, the CIA framework can serve as a basis for further understanding other key cybersecurity concepts and technologies, such as access controls, encryption, and data backup and recovery.

Board members should also be aware that the CIA framework is not a one-size-fits-all solution and that different types of data may require different levels of protection. For example, confidential financial data may require a higher level of protection than publicly available marketing materials.

Regarding confidentiality, board members should understand that this involves controlling access to sensitive data and ensuring that it is not disclosed to unauthorized individuals or entities. Examples could include employee personal data, financial information, trade secrets, or intellectual property.

For integrity, board members should understand that this involves ensuring that data is accurate, complete, and uncorrupted. Examples could include ensuring that financial data is not tampered with, customer orders are not changed, or medical records are not altered.

For availability, board members should understand that this involves ensuring that data and systems are accessible when needed. Examples could include ensuring that a website remains operational, customer service systems are available during business hours, or critical applications are not disrupted.

The CIA framework serves as a useful starting point for understanding the basic principles of cybersecurity and how they can be applied to protect a company's data and information. By understanding these principles, board members can better assess their company's cybersecurity risks and make informed decisions about how to mitigate them.

Cybersecurity Incident: Maersk

The Maersk NotPetya cyberattack in 2017 was one of the most significant cybersecurity incidents in recent history, with far-reaching consequences for the global shipping company and its board of directors. The attack targeted Maersk's IT infrastructure, resulting in the widespread disruption of operations and causing significant financial losses.

The impact on Maersk's board of directors was profound and required board members' immediate attention and involvement. The board had to make swift and critical decisions in response to the attack, including crisis management and strategic recovery efforts. The incident demanded members' leadership and guidance to navigate complex challenges and minimize the damage caused by the cyberattack.

The attack paralyzed the company's IT systems worldwide and, due to the essential role of Maersk in global shipping and logistics, affected its ability to operate efficiently and fulfill its obligations to customers. This created a severe disruption to the supply chain and caused significant financial losses, including direct costs for remediation, business interruption, and reputational damage.

The board of directors at Maersk had to mobilize quickly to assess the extent of the attack, understand its implications, and develop a comprehensive

(continued)

(continued)

response plan. Board members were responsible for coordinating efforts across various departments within the organization, engaging with external cybersecurity experts, and collaborating with relevant stakeholders to restore operations and minimize the impact on customers and partners.

The incident highlighted the critical importance of cyber resilience planning and proactive cybersecurity measures at the board level. It emphasized the need for robust security controls, incident response capabilities, and continuous monitoring and improvement of the company's cybersecurity posture. The board had to evaluate its cybersecurity strategy, assess potential vulnerabilities, and implement measures to prevent future attacks and enhance the company's resilience against cyber threats.

The Maersk NotPetya cyberattack served as a wake-up call for organizations across industries, demonstrating the potential consequences of cyberattacks on critical infrastructure. It reinforced the necessity for boards of directors to prioritize cybersecurity as a strategic business issue and allocate resources accordingly. The incident prompted Maersk's board to review and strengthen its cybersecurity governance practices, ensuring that cybersecurity risks and resilience were integrated into its overall business strategy.

The Maersk NotPetya cyberattack was a transformative event for the company's board of directors. It required board members to respond decisively to an unprecedented cybersecurity incident, emphasizing the importance of cyber resilience planning,

(continued)
crisis management, and strategic decision-making. The incident served as a valuable lesson for boards of directors worldwide, highlighting the imperative need of prioritizing cybersecurity and being prepared to handle and mitigate the potential consequences of cyberattacks on organizations.

Key Cybersecurity Concepts and Terminology for Board Members

Cybersecurity is a complex and technical field, and it can be challenging for board members to understand the many concepts and terminologies used in the industry. However, having a basic understanding of these key concepts is critical for effective cybersecurity governance. This section will provide an overview of some essential cybersecurity concepts and terminologies that board members should know.

Threats and Risks

A cybersecurity *threat* refers to the possibility or likelihood of an attack, breach, or intrusion on the organization's network, systems, and data by cybercriminals, hackers, or other malicious actors. These threats can take many forms, including malware, ransomware, phishing attacks, social engineering, and other tactics that seek to exploit vulnerabilities in an organization's cybersecurity defenses. The goal of a cybersecurity threat is to compromise the confidentiality, integrity, or availability of the organization's sensitive data or systems, which can result in significant financial, legal, and reputational damage.

A cybersecurity *risk* is the potential for a cyberattack or security breach to exploit a vulnerability in an organization's information systems or networks, leading to negative consequences, such as data loss, operational disruption, reputational damage, or financial losses. Cybersecurity risks can be categorized based on their likelihood and potential impact, and they can be mitigated through appropriate security controls and risk management strategies. Board members need to understand the cybersecurity risks facing their organization and the potential impact these risks can have on the company's operations, reputation, and financial health. By identifying and prioritizing cybersecurity risks, boards can work with management to implement effective risk management strategies and allocate resources to improve the organization's overall cybersecurity posture.

Vulnerabilities and Exploits

A cybersecurity *vulnerability* can be defined as a weakness or gap in an organization's security defenses that cyberattackers can exploit to gain unauthorized access, steal data, or disrupt operations. Vulnerabilities can exist in hardware, software, networks, processes, policies, or personnel. They can arise from various factors, such as software bugs, misconfigurations, weak passwords, lack of access controls, and social engineering attacks. Board members need to be aware of vulnerabilities and the risks they pose to the organization so that appropriate measures can be taken to mitigate them.

A cybersecurity *exploit* is a technique or method that takes advantage of a computer system or network vulnerability to gain unauthorized access or cause harm. It could involve a malicious actor using a piece of code or software to take advantage of a security weakness or vulnerability to compromise a system or steal data. Exploits can range from simple techniques to sophisticated attacks that use multiple vulnerabilities or methods. Board members need to understand cybersecurity exploits to properly evaluate the risks and implement effective controls to prevent and mitigate them.

Malware

Malware is any software designed to cause harm or compromise a system, including viruses, Trojans, worms, and ransomware:

- *Virus*: A type of malware that can replicate itself and infect other files or systems. Viruses can be spread through email, downloads, and other means and can cause a range of problems, from minor annoyances to serious system crashes and data loss.
- *Worm*: A self-replicating type of malware that can spread rapidly across a network or the Internet. Worms can be used for various purposes, such as data theft, denial-of-service attacks, or espionage.
- *Trojan*: A type of malware masquerading as a legitimate file or program to trick users into downloading or installing it. Once installed, Trojans can perform various malicious activities, such as stealing data, spying on user activity, or giving attackers remote access to the infected system.
- *Ransomware*: A type of malware that encrypts the victim's files or system, effectively locking them out of their own data or computer. The attacker then demands a ransom payment for the decryption key and may threaten to delete or publish the victim's data if they do not comply.
- *Adware*: A type of malware that displays unwanted advertisements or pop-ups on the victim's computer or mobile device. Adware is often bundled with legitimate software or downloads and can be difficult to remove once installed.

- *Spyware*: A type of malware that monitors the victim's computer activity, including keystrokes, web browsing, and file access. Spyware is often used for malicious purposes, such as stealing sensitive data or monitoring user behavior for targeted advertising or other purposes.
- *Rootkit*: A type of malware that hides its presence on the victim's computer or system, making it difficult to detect or remove. Rootkits can maintain persistent access to a system, steal data, or perform other malicious activities.
- *Keylogger*: A type of spyware that targets explicitly and records user keystrokes, often to steal login credentials, financial information, or other sensitive data. Keyloggers can be installed through phishing attacks, downloads, or other means and may be challenging to detect.

Social Engineering

Social engineering is a tactic used by threat actors to manipulate people into divulging confidential information or performing an action compromising a system or data:

- *Pretexting*: An attacker poses as someone else, such as a company representative, to gain access to sensitive information.
- *Phishing*: An attacker uses email or other electronic communication to trick individuals into divulging sensitive information or installing malware.
- *Spear phishing*: This is a more targeted form of phishing directed at specific individuals or organizations.
- *Vishing*: An attacker uses voice communication, such as a phone call, to trick individuals into divulging sensitive information.
- *Smishing*: An attacker uses text messages or other forms of mobile messaging to trick individuals into divulging sensitive information or installing malware.

- *Baiting*: An attacker leaves physical or digital bait, such as a USB drive, in a public place to entice someone to pick it up and plug it into their computer.
- *Quid pro quo*: An attacker promises a benefit in exchange for sensitive information or access.
- *Tailgating*: This is a physical social engineering attack that involves an attacker following someone into a secure area without authorization.
- *Watering hole*: An attacker compromises a website or other online resource that a target organization or individual frequently uses.

Encryption and Data Protection

Encryption is the process of converting data into a code that can be deciphered only with a key, making it unreadable to unauthorized parties:

- *Symmetric encryption*: A method of encryption in which the same key is used to encrypt and decrypt data. With symmetric encryption, the sender and receiver must have access to the same key to communicate securely.
- *Asymmetric encryption*: A method of encryption that uses two different keys: a public key and a private key. The public key is used to encrypt data, while the private key is used to decrypt it. This means data can be securely transmitted without the sender and receiver needing to share a common key.
- *Public key infrastructure (PKI)*: A set of technologies and practices used to establish and maintain a trusted network of digital certificates and public keys. PKI is used to secure communications between different parties and enable secure online transactions.
- *Digital signature*: A cryptographic mechanism used to verify the authenticity of a digital document or message. Digital signatures use a combination of hashing and

asymmetric encryption to ensure that a document has not been tampered with and originated from the sender it claims to come from.

- *Secure Sockets Layer/Transport Layer Security (SSL/TLS)*: SSL and TLS are cryptographic protocols used to secure Internet communications. These protocols provide encryption, authentication, and data integrity and are commonly used to secure online transactions, such as e-commerce and online banking. SSL has mostly been replaced by TLS, a newer and more secure protocol version.

Authentication and Access Control

Authentication is the process of verifying a user's identity through credentials, such as passwords, biometric data, or smart cards. Access controls consist of several elements:

- *Authorization*: The process of granting or denying access to a user or system based on their level of permissions.
- *Multifactor authentication (MFA)*: A security mechanism that requires users to provide multiple forms of identification to access a system, network, or application. Typically, MFA requires users to provide two or more factors, such as a password, fingerprint, or security token, to confirm their identity and access the system.
- *Single sign-on (SSO)*: An authentication process that enables users to access multiple applications and systems with a single set of login credentials. This means users have to sign in only once to access all the resources they need, rather than having to sign in to each separately.
- *Privileged access management (PAM)*: A security solution that helps organizations manage and monitor access to their most critical systems and data. PAM systems typically include features, such as access controls, password management, and session monitoring and are designed

to provide a secure and auditable way for administrators to manage privileged accounts.

- *Role-based access control (RBAC)*: A method of controlling access to systems and applications based on users' roles within an organization. Rather than assigning permissions to individual users, RBAC systems assign permissions based on the user's job function or role. This allows organizations to manage access more efficiently and securely and helps ensure that users only have access to the resources they need to do their job.

It's essential for board members to have a basic understanding of these key cybersecurity concepts and terminologies. In the following sections, we will discuss how these concepts apply to the specific challenges faced by SMBs and provide guidance on how board members can use this knowledge to improve their cybersecurity governance.

Cybersecurity Incident: LinkedIn

In May 2021, LinkedIn faced a significant data breach, resulting in the exposure of more than 700 million users' personal information. The data included users' full names, email addresses, phone numbers, and other details. The company confirmed that the data was scraped from its website and other online sources, including information that was already publicly available. However, despite the company's attempts to downplay the significance of the breach, some experts have raised concerns about potential misuse of the data by threat actors. It is still being determined how the company's board of directors has responded to the incident.

Common Cyber Threats and Risks Faced by Companies

In today's world, cyber threats are ever-evolving and increasingly sophisticated, and board members must be aware of the most common cyber threats and risks that companies face. This section will discuss some of the most prevalent cyber threats and risks that SMBs encounter and their potential impact on the company.

Phishing

Phishing is a type of cyberattack in which attackers try to obtain sensitive information from individuals or organizations by tricking them into clicking a link or providing login credentials. Typically, phishing emails are designed to look like they come from a trusted source, such as a bank or other financial institution, a vendor, or even the individual's employer.

For board members, it is important to understand the potential impact of phishing attacks on the organization, including the loss of sensitive information and the potential for financial loss. It is also important to understand that while technology solutions, such as email filters and firewalls, can help mitigate the risk of phishing attacks, training and awareness programs for employees are also critical to ensure that they are able to recognize and avoid these types of attacks.

Board members should work with management to ensure that the organization has a comprehensive training and awareness program in place for all employees. This program should include regular training on how to identify and avoid phishing attacks, as well as simulated phishing attacks to test the program's effectiveness. In addition, board members should ensure that the organization has policies and procedures to respond to and mitigate the impact of a successful phishing attack, including a plan for quickly identifying and isolating the affected systems and procedures for notifying customers or other affected parties.

Board members can also work with management to ensure that the organization has the appropriate technology solutions in place to help detect and mitigate the risk of phishing attacks. These may include email filtering solutions, as well as endpoint security solutions that can help detect and prevent the installation of malware as a result of a phishing attack. Finally, board members should ensure that the organization has appropriate incident response plans to quickly respond to and recover from a successful phishing attack.

Malware

As a board member, it's important to understand the risks and impact of malware on a company's cybersecurity. *Malware* (short for *malicious software*) refers to any software designed to harm, exploit, or infiltrate a computer system without the user's knowledge or consent. Malware can come in many different forms, including viruses, Trojans, worms, ransomware, adware, spyware, rootkits, and keyloggers.

Malware can be used to steal sensitive information, such as customer data, intellectual property, or financial records, and can also be used to cause operational disruptions or financial harm to a company. For example, ransomware attacks can encrypt a company's data and demand payment in exchange for the decryption key. Malware can also be used to create backdoors or remote access points to a company's network, allowing attackers to launch further attacks or steal sensitive data.

As a board member, it's important to ensure that the company has proper protections in place to detect and prevent malware attacks. These may include implementing antivirus and anti-malware software, performing regular software updates and patching, limiting employee access to sensitive data, and providing employee education and training on best practices for identifying and avoiding potential malware threats.

In addition, it's important to have an incident response plan in case of a malware attack. The plan should include procedures for identifying and containing the attack, communicating with relevant stakeholders, conducting a forensic investigation, and implementing remediation measures to prevent future attacks.

Board members should also ensure that the company is conducting regular security assessments and audits to identify potential vulnerabilities and address any issues in a timely manner. By staying informed and involved in the company's cybersecurity efforts, board members can help minimize the risk of malware and other cybersecurity threats.

Ransomware

As a board member, it is important to be aware of the growing threat of ransomware attacks. *Ransomware* is a type of malicious software (malware) designed to block access to a computer system or data until a ransom is paid. Ransomware attacks have become increasingly common in recent years and can have significant consequences for businesses and organizations.

One of the main risks of a ransomware attack is the potential loss of critical data or intellectual property, which can result in operational disruptions and reputational damage. Additionally, the cost of responding to a ransomware attack can be high, including restoring systems, paying the ransom, and conducting forensic investigations.

Board members should ensure that their organization has appropriate policies and procedures to prevent and respond to ransomware attacks. This includes implementing strong security controls and regularly backing up critical data. It is also important to have an incident response plan that outlines the steps to take in the event of a ransomware attack, including how to isolate infected systems and negotiate with attackers.

In addition, board members should ensure that their organization has appropriate cyber insurance coverage, which can help mitigate the financial impact of a ransomware attack. However, it is important to note that paying the ransom is not recommended, as it may encourage further attacks and does not guarantee that the data will be restored.

Business Email Compromise

Business email compromise (BEC) is a type of cyberattack that targets businesses and organizations through email communication. The goal of this attack is to compromise an email account and use it to fraudulently request a wire transfer or payment to a fraudulent account. BEC attacks are also known as *CEO fraud* or *whaling* attacks.

In a BEC attack, the attacker first gains access to a legitimate email account through any of a variety of methods, such as social engineering or phishing, or by exploiting a vulnerability in the email system. Once they have access, the attacker can impersonate the email account owner and send an email that appears to come from a trusted source, such as the CEO or another high-level executive.

The email usually contains urgent or sensitive language requesting a wire transfer or payment to a specific account. The account provided by the attacker is typically a fraudulent account controlled by the attacker.

BEC attacks can be difficult to detect because they often involve a high degree of social engineering and impersonation. They can also be sophisticated, using techniques, such as email spoofing and domain name impersonation to make the email appear legitimate.

Board members should be aware of the potential for BEC attacks and ensure that their organization has proper security measures in place to detect and prevent these types of attacks. These include training employees to recognize phishing and other social engineering tactics, implementing strong email security protocols, and using multifactor authentication for sensitive accounts.

In addition, board members should be aware of the potential financial and reputational damage that can result from a successful BEC attack. It is important to have a response plan in case of a breach, including communication protocols and a plan for recovery and remediation.

Insider Threats

An *insider threat* is a cybersecurity risk that comes from within an organization, such as an employee or contractor with access to sensitive information or systems. Insider threats can take many forms, including intentional malicious activity, unintentional mistakes, or negligence.

For a board member, it is important to understand the risks associated with insider threats and ensure that appropriate measures are in place to mitigate those risks. These include policies and procedures to prevent or detect insider threats, such as background checks, security awareness training, access controls, monitoring and auditing of user activity, and incident response plans.

Board members should also be aware that insider threats can come from all levels of the organization, including senior executives, and that these individuals may have access to particularly sensitive information or systems. Therefore, it is important to ensure that appropriate oversight and controls are in place and senior executives are held to the same security standards as other employees.

Finally, board members should be aware that insider threats can be particularly difficult to detect and prevent, as insiders may have legitimate access to the systems or information they are targeting. Therefore, it is important to have a comprehensive cybersecurity program that includes a range of security controls and ongoing monitoring and testing to identify potential vulnerabilities and threats.

Third-Party Risk

As businesses continue to increase their reliance on third-party vendors and partners for various services, the risks associated with these relationships also increase. Board members must understand the potential risks that third-party vendors and partners pose to their organization's cybersecurity.

First, board members should understand that third-party risks can come in many forms. For example, a third-party vendor may be hacked or compromised in some way, potentially exposing sensitive data belonging to the organization. Additionally, a third-party vendor may not have adequate security measures in place to protect the organization's data, potentially leading to a breach or other cybersecurity incident.

Board members should also understand that the risks associated with third-party vendors are not limited to data security. A third-party vendor could also pose risks related to business continuity, as the vendor may be a critical part of the organization's operations. If the third-party vendor experiences an outage or other disruption, it could significantly impact the organization's ability to operate.

To mitigate third-party risks, board members should ensure that their organization has a comprehensive third-party risk management program. This program should include processes for assessing and monitoring the cybersecurity risks associated with each third-party vendor and partner, as well as processes for taking action when risks are identified.

Board members should also ensure that their organization has contracts with each third-party vendor that clearly outline the vendor's responsibilities for protecting the organization's data and systems. These contracts should include provisions related to data security, business continuity, and incident response.

Finally, board members should ensure that their organization has adequate resources allocated to managing third-party risks. These include personnel with the skills and expertise to manage vendor relationships, as well as technologies and other tools to monitor vendor activities and detect potential cybersecurity risks.

Mistakes/Errors

As a board member, it is important to be aware that mistakes and errors can pose a significant cybersecurity risk to the organization. Even the best-designed security systems and protocols can be rendered useless by a single mistake or error made by an employee or contractor.

One of the most common sources of mistakes and errors is human error. Employees and contractors may accidentally click a malicious link or attachment in an email, visit a malicious website, or leave a device with sensitive information unsecured. Other sources of mistakes and errors may include inadequate training and awareness of cybersecurity risks, poor password management practices, or failure to follow established security policies and procedures.

As a result, board members should ensure that their organization has effective cybersecurity training programs for all employees and contractors. Such training should be designed to raise awareness of common cybersecurity risks and provide practical guidance on mitigating those risks. Additionally, board members should ensure that their organization has policies and procedures to prevent common cybersecurity errors, such as requiring multifactor authentication and ensuring that all devices are encrypted.

It is also important for board members to recognize that mistakes and errors may occur as a result of the organization's own processes and systems. For example, an organization may fail to update its software or hardware regularly, leaving it vulnerable to known exploits. In such cases, it is important to identify and address such vulnerabilities promptly and establish procedures to prevent similar issues from occurring in the future.

As a board member, it is essential to be aware of the potential risks associated with mistakes and errors in cybersecurity. The best way to mitigate these risks is to implement effective training programs and security policies and procedures while also regularly assessing and updating the organization's systems and processes.

It's essential for board members to be aware of the most common cyber threats and risks companies face. By understanding these threats and their potential impact, board members can take the necessary steps to mitigate risk and protect the company from cyberattacks. The following sections will guide board members in managing these risks and developing effective cybersecurity strategies for their company.

Emerging Threats

As technology continues to advance, so do the tactics of cyberattackers. While many companies focus on defending against known threats, it is important for board members to be aware of emerging cyber threats as well. The following are some of the most significant emerging cyber threats.

Advanced Persistent Threats

Advanced persistent threats (APTs) are sophisticated cyber-attacks typically carried out by highly skilled and well-funded attackers, such as nation-state actors, organized crime groups, or advanced hacking groups. APTs are often characterized by their ability to evade detection and remain hidden within a targeted network for long periods, sometimes months or even years:

- Board members should be aware that APTs are among the most serious and persistent threats to their organization's cybersecurity and can have devastating consequences if not detected and remediated promptly. APTs are often designed to steal sensitive data or disrupt critical business operations, which can result in significant financial and reputational damage to the organization.
- To protect against APTs, board members should ensure that their organization has implemented robust cybersecurity measures, including strong access controls, network segmentation, and continuous monitoring and threat detection. Additionally, board members should ensure that their organization has an effective incident response plan so it is prepared to quickly and effectively respond to an APT attack if one occurs.
- Board members should also be aware that APTs are constantly evolving, with new tactics and techniques emerging regularly. To stay ahead of these threats, board members should prioritize ongoing cybersecurity education and training for all employees, as well as regular cybersecurity assessments and testing to identify vulnerabilities and weaknesses in their organization's security posture. Finally, board members should stay up to date on the latest APT trends and emerging threat vectors and ensure that their organization's cybersecurity strategy is regularly reviewed and updated to address new and evolving threats.

Supply Chain Attacks

As a board member, it is important to understand the risk of *supply chain attacks* and the potential impact on the organization. A supply chain attack occurs when a hacker targets a vendor, supplier, or another third-party service provider to gain access to an organization's network or data. In other words, a supply chain attack takes advantage of vulnerabilities in the security practices of the organization's partners or vendors.

A supply chain attack can occur in several ways, including the following:

- *Compromised software*: Hackers can embed malware into legitimate software and distribute it through the supply chain. When the target organization installs the software, the malware is activated and can allow the attacker to gain unauthorized access to the system.
- *Third-party credentials*: Attackers can obtain login credentials from a vendor or supplier and use them to access the target organization's systems.
- *Hardware tampering*: Hackers can manipulate hardware components, such as routers or servers, during the manufacturing process to insert malware that can be used to compromise the system.

Supply chain attacks can have a devastating impact on an organization, including the loss of sensitive data, financial loss, and damage to the company's reputation. It is important for board members to ensure that their organization has strong security practices and that their vendors and partners follow similar practices.

To mitigate the risk of supply chain attacks, board members should do the following:

- *Conduct due diligence on third-party vendors and suppliers.* Before partnering with a vendor or supplier, board members should ensure that the vendor or supplier has strong security practices in place.

- *Implement strong security practices.* Organizations should have a comprehensive cybersecurity program that includes measures, such as multifactor authentication, network segmentation, and encryption.
- *Monitor for potential threats.* Board members should ensure that their organization has robust monitoring capabilities to detect any potential threats, such as anomalous activity from a vendor or supplier.
- *Develop an incident response plan.* In the event of a supply chain attack, board members should ensure that their organization has an incident response plan to minimize the impact of the attack and quickly recover.

Data Destruction

Data destruction cyberattacks, also known as *data wiping* or *data erasure* attacks, are a type of cyberattack where the attacker deliberately destroys or corrupts data. This is often done by overwriting data with random or meaningless data, rendering the original data unreadable and irrecoverable:

- Board members should be aware of the risks of data destruction attacks and take steps to ensure that their company's data is protected. This can involve implementing strong access controls and regularly backing up critical data to a secure off-site location. It is also important to have a robust incident response plan with steps for recovering from a data destruction attack, including restoring data from backups and identifying the source of the attack.
- Data destruction attacks can have serious consequences, including lost or damaged data, financial losses, and damage to a company's reputation. Board members should work with their IT and security teams to ensure

that their organization has the necessary controls and procedures to mitigate the risk of such attacks.

Zero-Day Exploits

A *zero-day exploit* is a type of cyberattack that takes advantage of a software vulnerability that is unknown to the software developer or vendor. Attackers can exploit this vulnerability to gain unauthorized access to computer systems or data. The term *zero-day* refers to the fact that the vulnerability is unknown and has not been patched, giving attackers a head start:

- Board members should be aware that zero-day exploits are a significant threat to the cybersecurity of their organization, as such attacks can be difficult to detect and defend against. These exploits can be used to spread malware, steal sensitive data, or even take control of an entire network.
- To protect against zero-day exploits, board members should ensure that their organization has robust cybersecurity measures in place, including up-to-date software and firmware, firewalls, intrusion detection and prevention systems, and regular security audits. They should also encourage a culture of cybersecurity awareness and education among employees, as human error can often be a weak link in an organization's security defenses.
- It's important for board members to stay informed about emerging zero-day exploits and new cybersecurity threats in general, as the threat landscape is constantly evolving. They should work closely with their IT and security teams to ensure that their organization is prepared to respond quickly and effectively to any emerging threats and that they have a well-defined incident response plan in place.

Internet of Things Attacks

As more devices become connected to the Internet, the potential attack surface for cybercriminals is growing. The Internet of Things (IoT) is a network of devices, vehicles, and home appliances that contain sensors, software, and network connectivity, allowing them to collect and exchange data. This interconnectedness presents a new set of security risks for organizations, which can be particularly concerning for board members.

One of the main risks associated with IoT devices is their vulnerability to attack. Many IoT devices are not designed with security in mind, and the rush to bring new products to market often means security is an afterthought. As a result, many IoT devices are poorly secured, making them easy targets for cybercriminals.

IoT attacks can take many different forms, including the following:

- *Botnets*: A botnet is a network of compromised computers or IoT devices that can be used to launch distributed denial-of-service (DDoS) attacks or steal sensitive data.
- *Ransomware*: Cybercriminals can use IoT devices as an entry point to launch ransomware attacks, where they encrypt a victim's files and demand payment in exchange for the decryption key.
- *Data theft*: IoT devices can be used to collect sensitive data, such as credit card information, and transmit it back to cybercriminals.
- *Physical damage*: Certain types of IoT devices, such as industrial control systems, can be used to cause physical damage, such as shutting down critical infrastructure or causing explosions.

To protect against IoT attacks, board members should work with their IT and security teams to develop a comprehensive security strategy that addresses the unique risks associated with IoT devices. This may involve developing policies and procedures for IoT device management, such as patching and updating devices, using strong authentication, and monitoring devices for suspicious activity. Additionally, organizations should consider using network segmentation to separate IoT devices from critical systems and implementing robust access controls to limit the impact of a potential IoT attack.

Cloud Security

As more companies move their data and applications to the cloud, board members need to understand the security risks and challenges associated with cloud computing. Here are some key things a board member should know about cloud security:

- *Shared responsibility model*: In cloud computing, a shared responsibility model exists between the cloud service provider and the customer. The provider is responsible for securing the infrastructure, while the customer is responsible for securing the applications, data, and users. Board members should ensure that their organization clearly understands its responsibilities in the cloud.
- *Data protection*: Data stored in the cloud is often spread across multiple servers and data centers. This can make it difficult to ensure the security and privacy of sensitive data. Board members should ensure that their organization has appropriate data protection measures in place, such as encryption and access controls.
- *Identity and access management*: Cloud services can be accessed from anywhere, so access to data and applications needs to be carefully controlled. Board members should ensure that their organization has strong identity and access management policies and procedures to prevent unauthorized access.

- *Compliance*: Cloud computing can introduce additional compliance challenges, especially when it comes to data residency and data privacy regulations. Board members should ensure that their organization is aware of the compliance requirements for its industry and has measures in place to meet those requirements.
- *Incident response*: In the event of a security incident in the cloud, it can be more difficult to determine the extent of the damage and respond effectively. Board members should ensure that their organization has an effective incident response plan that includes procedures for responding to security incidents in the cloud.
- *Third-party security*: Many cloud services rely on third-party providers for services, such as storage, content delivery, and security. Board members should ensure that their organization has appropriate contracts and agreements with these providers to be sure their security measures are adequate.
- *Continuous monitoring*: Cloud security is not a one-time effort but requires continuous monitoring and improvement. Board members should ensure that their organization has appropriate monitoring tools and processes to detect and respond to security threats in the cloud.

Board members should ensure that their organization has a comprehensive and effective cloud security strategy that addresses the unique risks and challenges of cloud computing.

Mobile Device Security

As mobile devices have become increasingly prevalent in the workplace, mobile device security has become a critical concern for companies. Board members should understand the risks associated with the use of mobile devices and the measures that can be taken to mitigate these risks.

One of the key risks associated with mobile devices is the potential for them to be lost or stolen. If a device that contains sensitive company information is lost or stolen, this could result in a significant data breach. Companies can mitigate this risk by implementing strong device encryption and requiring employees to use complex passwords to access their devices.

Another risk associated with mobile devices is the use of unsecured public Wi-Fi networks. When employees use these networks to access company data, it increases the risk of data interception and compromise. Board members should understand the importance of using virtual private networks (VPNs) when accessing company data from public Wi-Fi networks.

In addition, board members should be aware of the risks associated with using third-party apps on mobile devices. These apps can potentially access sensitive company data and may not have the same level of security as the company's internal systems. To mitigate this risk, companies can implement policies and procedures around the use of third-party apps on mobile devices.

Finally, board members should understand the importance of keeping mobile devices up to date with the latest security patches and updates. Outdated software can contain vulnerabilities that attackers can exploit. Companies should have policies and procedures to ensure that mobile devices are regularly updated with the latest security patches.

In summary, board members should be aware of the risks associated with mobile devices and the measures that can be taken to mitigate these risks. By implementing strong security measures, companies can ensure that mobile devices are used safely and securely in the workplace.

Key Technologies and Defense Strategies

The following are key technologies that board members should be familiar with to better understand cybersecurity risks and defenses.

Firewall Technology

A *firewall* is a network security device that monitors and controls incoming and outgoing network traffic based on predefined security rules. It acts as a barrier between a company's internal network and the external Internet, allowing only authorized traffic to pass through while blocking unauthorized traffic.

Firewalls work by examining incoming traffic and comparing it against predefined rules to determine whether it is allowed. If traffic is allowed, the firewall allows it to pass through to the network. If traffic is not allowed, the firewall blocks it and prevents it from reaching its destination.

There are several different types of firewalls, including the following:

- *Packet filtering firewalls*: Examine individual data packets and compare them against a set of predefined rules
- *Stateful inspection firewalls*: Examine each incoming packet in the context of previous packets, allowing for more advanced filtering
- *Application-level gateways*: Examine the content of packets, including the application layer data, and make decisions based on the specific application being used
- *Next-generation firewalls*: Use advanced technologies, such as intrusion prevention, antivirus software, and URL filtering, to provide more comprehensive protection

Some of the most popular vendors of firewall technology include:

- *Cisco*: A well-known provider of network infrastructure, including firewalls
- *Palo Alto Networks*: A provider of next-generation firewalls that use advanced technologies to provide more comprehensive protection
- *Fortinet*: A provider of security solutions, including firewalls, designed to protect against a range of cyber threats
- *Check Point*: A provider of firewall and security solutions for both on-premises and cloud-based environments
- *Juniper Networks*: A provider of network and security solutions, including firewalls, designed to provide secure access and protection for enterprise networks

Board members should be aware of the importance of firewalls in protecting their company's network from unauthorized access and cyberattacks. They should work with their IT and cybersecurity teams to ensure that the company has appropriate firewall technology in place and that it is configured and maintained properly.

Intrusion Detection/Prevention Systems

Intrusion detection systems/intrusion prevention systems (IDSs/IPSs) are technologies designed to detect and prevent unauthorized access to computer networks. An IDS monitors and analyzes network traffic to detect signs of an attack, while an IPS goes one step further by actively blocking the attack. These technologies help protect against cyber threats, such as viruses, malware, and hacking attempts.

An IDS/IPS can be host-based or network-based. Host-based systems operate on individual computers and protect against attacks targeting that specific system, while network-based systems operate on the network level and protect against attacks targeting multiple systems.

Some popular vendors of IDS/IPS technology include Cisco, Fortinet, McAfee, and Palo Alto Networks. These companies offer a range of products with varying capabilities, including cloud-based options and managed services.

Board members should be aware of the importance of IDS/IPS technology in protecting their company's network and data. By implementing an IDS/IPS, the company can monitor and prevent unauthorized access, detect and block cyber threats in real time, and minimize the impact of security incidents. It is important for board members to work with their IT and security teams to select the appropriate IDS/IPS solution for their organization and ensure that it is regularly updated and maintained to stay effective against evolving cyber threats.

Encryption

Encryption is a process of converting plain text or data into a code or cipher to protect the confidentiality of information. It involves using mathematical algorithms to scramble information so that it can be read only by someone with the key or password to unlock it. Encryption is an essential part of modern cybersecurity and is used to protect sensitive data in transit and data at rest on storage devices.

There are two primary types of encryption: symmetric and asymmetric. Symmetric encryption uses the same key for encryption and decryption, while asymmetric encryption uses two keys, a public key for encryption and a private key for decryption. Asymmetric encryption is commonly used in secure communication protocols like SSL and TLS.

Encryption can be implemented at various levels in an IT infrastructure, from the application layer to the network layer. Data encryption software can be used to encrypt files, folders, and disks, while email encryption tools can be used to encrypt messages and attachments. Full-disk encryption can be used to encrypt an entire storage device, and encryption can also be implemented at the network layer to secure communication channels.

Some popular encryption technology vendors include Microsoft BitLocker, McAfee Endpoint Encryption, Symantec Endpoint Encryption, VeraCrypt, and AxCrypt.

Board members should have a basic understanding of encryption and its importance in protecting sensitive data. Encryption is critical to cybersecurity and can help prevent data breaches and unauthorized access to sensitive information. Board members should be aware of the types of encryption used by their organization and ensure that proper encryption protocols are in place to protect data at rest and in transit. Additionally, they should stay informed about advancements in encryption technology and consider implementing new encryption technologies as appropriate.

Multifactor Authentication

This technology requires users to provide more than one form of authentication to access a system or network, making it more difficult for hackers to gain access through stolen passwords. Board members should understand how multifactor authentication (MFA) works and its benefits in protecting company systems.

MFA is a security mechanism that requires users to provide multiple forms of identification before being granted access to a system or application. This technology offers an extra layer of security by requiring more than just a username and password to access a system, reducing the risk of unauthorized access due to stolen or weak credentials.

MFA typically requires the user to provide two or more of the following: something they know (such as a password), something they have (such as a security token or mobile device), or something they are (such as a fingerprint or other biometric data). The specific authentication methods used can vary depending on the organization's security policies and the systems being accessed.

MFA can be implemented in various ways, including through hardware tokens, software tokens, SMS-based codes, push notifications, or biometric data. Some of the most popular vendors of MFA technology include RSA, Okta, Duo Security, Microsoft Azure Active Directory, and Google Authenticator.

Board members should be aware of the importance of MFA in protecting sensitive information and reducing the risk of cyberattacks. By requiring multiple forms of authentication, the company can significantly increase the security of its systems and prevent unauthorized access by bad actors. Additionally, board members should understand how MFA can be implemented in their company's specific technology environment and which vendors may be most suitable for their needs.

Virtual Private Network

A *virtual private network* (VPN) is a technology that allows users to securely connect to a remote network over the public Internet. VPNs use encryption and authentication to ensure that data transmitted over the Internet is protected from interception and tampering.

A VPN works by creating a secure, encrypted connection between a user's device and a remote server or network. The user's device sends data to the remote server or network through this encrypted connection, ensuring that it cannot be intercepted or modified by unauthorized parties. The remote server or network then decrypts the data and sends it to its final destination.

VPNs can provide secure remote access to a company's internal network for employees working from home or on the road. They can also connect geographically distributed offices and enable secure communication between them.

Popular vendors of VPN technology include Cisco, Palo Alto Networks, Fortinet, and Check Point. These vendors provide a range of VPN solutions, including software-based VPN clients and hardware-based VPN gateways. It's important for companies to choose a reputable vendor and ensure that their VPN solution is properly configured and managed to ensure maximum security.

Antivirus and Anti-malware Software

Antivirus and anti-malware software are computer programs designed to protect against malicious software, also known as *malware*. Malware is a type of software that is designed to harm or exploit a computer system, network, or device. Malware includes viruses, worms, Trojans, spyware, adware, and other types of malicious code.

Antivirus and anti-malware software is designed to detect and remove malware from computers and other devices. They work by scanning files and programs on the device for known patterns or signatures of malware. When malware is detected, the software can either quarantine or delete the infected files or programs.

Some of the most popular vendors of antivirus and anti-malware software include the following:

- Norton by Symantec
- McAfee by Intel Security
- Avast
- AVG Technologies
- Kaspersky Lab
- ESET

- Trend Micro
- Sophos
- Bitdefender
- Malwarebytes

Board members should be aware that while antivirus and anti-malware software can effectively detect and remove known malware, it is not foolproof. Cybercriminals are constantly developing new and sophisticated forms of malware that may not be detected by traditional antivirus and anti-malware software. Therefore, it is important to use other security measures besides antivirus and anti-malware software, such as firewalls, intrusion detection and prevention systems, and regular software updates and patching.

Endpoint Detection and Response

Endpoint detection and response (EDR) technology is a cybersecurity solution designed to detect and respond to endpoint threats, such as desktops, laptops, servers, and mobile devices. EDR tools are used to monitor and analyze endpoint activity continuously, and they are designed to detect and respond to advanced threats that may bypass traditional security measures, such as firewalls and antivirus software.

EDR solutions typically use a combination of signature-based and behavior-based detection techniques. They rely on data collected from endpoints to identify indicators of compromise and use machine learning and other advanced analytics techniques to detect anomalous behavior and activity patterns that may indicate an attack.

Once an EDR solution identifies a threat, it can respond in several ways, including blocking the threat, quarantining an infected device, or providing detailed information to security analysts to aid in their investigation and response. EDR solutions may also include automated remediation features, automatically containing and removing threats from an infected endpoint.

Popular EDR vendors include CrowdStrike, Carbon Black, FireEye, Symantec, and Trend Micro.

Patch Management

Patch management is the process of identifying, acquiring, installing, and verifying patches or updates to software applications and systems to address known vulnerabilities and ensure that they are secure. Software vendors release these patches to address security vulnerabilities, bugs, and other issues identified in their software products.

Patch management is important because hackers can exploit vulnerabilities to gain unauthorized access to computer systems, steal sensitive data, and cause other types of damage. By applying patches, companies can reduce the risk of a security breach.

Some popular patch management solutions include Microsoft's Windows Server Update Services (WSUS), IBM's BigFix, and SolarWinds Patch Manager. These solutions automate the process of identifying and deploying patches to devices across a company's network, reducing the time and effort required to keep systems up to date and secure.

Board members should be aware of patch management as a critical aspect of cybersecurity and understand the importance of keeping systems and software up to date to protect against potential security breaches. They should also ensure that their company has a plan to manage patches and updates and that the plan is regularly reviewed and updated to address emerging threats and vulnerabilities.

Cloud Technology

Cloud technology refers to using remote servers to store, manage, and process data and applications over the Internet rather than using local or on-premises infrastructure. This approach allows organizations to access computing resources and services on demand, pay only for what they use, and scale their operations as needed.

From a cybersecurity standpoint, cloud technology can introduce new risks, such as unauthorized access, data breaches, and misconfigured security controls. However, when implemented correctly, cloud technology can improve an organizations' security posture by taking advantage of the expertise and resources of cloud service providers.

Organizations need to implement robust security controls to protect their cloud-based assets, such as access management, encryption, and network segmentation. They should also ensure that their cloud service providers have appropriate security measures, such as data encryption, vulnerability management, and incident response.

The most popular cloud service providers include Amazon Web Services (AWS), Microsoft Azure, and Google Cloud Platform. These providers offer a range of cloud-based services, including infrastructure as a service (IaaS), platform as a service (PaaS), and software as a service (SaaS) products. Additionally, several third-party security vendors offer tools and services specifically designed to enhance the security of cloud environments, such as cloud access security brokers (CASBs) and cloud workload protection platforms (CWPPs).

Identity and Access Management

Identity and Access Management (IAM) is a framework of policies and technologies for ensuring secure and appropriate access to systems and data. It involves managing user identities, enforcing access policies, and tracking user activity to reduce the risk of unauthorized access or data breaches.

IAM systems are typically used to provide access control to networks, applications, and data, as well as to enforce policies related to password management, user roles and permissions, and multifactor authentication. The aim is to ensure that only authorized users can access sensitive information and that their actions are logged and auditable.

Popular IAM vendors include Microsoft Azure Active Directory, Okta, OneLogin, and Ping Identity. These vendors offer various IAM solutions, including identity governance and administration, multifactor authentication, and privileged access management. IAM solutions are typically cloud-based, which makes them more accessible and easier to manage for companies of all sizes.

Board members should be familiar with IAM concepts and technologies, as IAM is a critical aspect of a comprehensive cybersecurity program. IAM solutions can help prevent unauthorized access to sensitive data, reduce the risk of data breaches, and improve the organization's overall security posture. Additionally, board members should ensure that the IAM solution is aligned with the company's cybersecurity strategy, policies, and compliance requirements.

Mobile Device Management

Mobile device management (MDM) technology is a type of software that enables companies to secure, monitor, and manage mobile devices, such as smartphones and tablets, used by employees. With the proliferation of mobile devices in the workplace, it has become increasingly important for companies to have the ability to control access to corporate data and applications on these devices, as well as to enforce security policies.

MDM solutions allow companies to remotely manage and secure mobile devices from a central console and provide a range of features, such as the following:

- *Device enrollment and configuration*: MDM solutions can automatically enroll new devices, configure security policies, and push updates and apps to devices.
- *Device monitoring and control*: MDM solutions can monitor device usage and enforce security policies, such as requiring device passcodes or remotely wiping devices in the event of loss or theft.
- *Application management*: MDM solutions can control which apps are allowed on devices and can push updates or remove apps remotely.
- *Content management*: MDM solutions can control access to corporate data and provide secure access to email, files, and other content on devices.

Some popular MDM vendors include the following:

- VMware AirWatch
- Microsoft Intune
- IBM MaaS360
- MobileIron
- Citrix Endpoint Management
- BlackBerry UEM

Board members should be aware of the importance of MDM solutions in securing mobile devices used by employees and ensure that their company has an effective MDM strategy in place. They should also be aware of the risks associated with employees using personal devices for work purposes and consider implementing a bring-your-own-device (BYOD) policy to manage these risks.

Data Backup and Recovery

Data backup and recovery technology is an essential component of any cybersecurity strategy. It involves creating copies of important data and storing them securely to enable their recovery in case of data loss due to cyberattacks, natural disasters, or human error.

Data backup involves making a duplicate copy of data, either on-premises or in the cloud. This copy can be created manually or automatically and can be performed regularly, such as daily or weekly. The backup data can be stored in different formats, such as on hard drives, on tapes, or in the cloud, and can be encrypted to ensure its confidentiality.

Data recovery is the process of restoring data from a backup after a cyberattack or other incident causes data loss or corruption. Recovery involves copying the backed-up data to the original location or another location as needed. The process can involve a range of tools and techniques, including backup software, restoration tools, and recovery processes.

There are several popular vendors of data backup and recovery technology, including the following:

- *Veeam*: Provides a variety of backup and recovery solutions for virtual, physical, and cloud-based environments
- *Commvault*: Offers backup and recovery solutions for cloud, virtual, and physical data, with features, such as data deduplication and disaster recovery
- *Acronis*: Offers a range of data backup and recovery solutions for businesses, including backup and recovery for endpoints, servers, and virtual environments
- *Rubrik*: Provides a cloud-based data management platform that includes backup, recovery, and cloud archival
- *Veritas*: Offers a comprehensive data protection solution, including backup and recovery, archiving, and disaster recovery

Board members should be aware of the importance of data backup and recovery technology, as it is critical for ensuring business continuity and mitigating the impact of cyberattacks. They should also be aware of the key features and capabilities of popular backup and recovery solutions, as well as the benefits and risks associated with each technology. This understanding will help them to make informed decisions about cybersecurity investments and strategies to protect the company's data and assets.

Zero-Trust Architecture

Zero-trust architecture is an approach to cybersecurity that assumes no level of trust for any users, devices, or networks, regardless of whether they are inside or outside the organization's perimeter. In a zero-trust architecture, every resource and access request is verified, authenticated, and authorized before it is granted.

The zero-trust architecture model focuses on the identity of the user, device, and application. Instead of granting broad access privileges, the model provides the least access possible to complete a task based on a user's need to know. For example, access to sensitive data is granted only to those who have been explicitly authorized and authenticated.

This approach is based on the belief that security breaches can occur from both outside and inside the organization, and therefore, every device and user, whether internal or external, must be authenticated and authorized to access resources. Zero-trust architecture relies on strong authentication, encryption, and segmentation to protect against cyber threats.

Popular vendors that offer zero-trust solutions include Cisco, Microsoft, Palo Alto Networks, and Google. These vendors offer solutions that use a combination of various technologies, such as identity and access management, multifactor authentication, and micro-segmentation, to enforce the zero-trust model.

Micro-segmentation

Micro-segmentation is a cybersecurity technology that enables a company to divide its network into smaller, independently secured or controlled micro-segments. This helps minimize the spread of cyber threats and reduce the impact of a potential breach by containing it within a specific area of the network.

Micro-segmentation works by creating virtual boundaries around different parts of the network, allowing administrators to control access and limit data movement between different segments. This makes it harder for cybercriminals to move laterally within the network and access sensitive data or systems.

One popular implementation of micro-segmentation is using software-defined networking (SDN) technology, which allows the network to be programmatically managed and dynamically adjusted. Another implementation is through virtualization technologies, which enable the creation of isolated virtual networks within the physical network infrastructure.

Some popular vendors that offer micro-segmentation technology include VMware with their product NSX, Cisco with their product ACI, Illumio, Guardicore, and Unisys.

Board members should understand the benefits of micro-segmentation and how it can be used to improve their company's cybersecurity posture. By implementing micro-segmentation, companies can enhance their overall security posture and reduce the impact of a cyberattack by limiting the movement of a threat across the network. Additionally, micro-segmentation can provide greater visibility into network traffic and enable more granular control of access to data and systems.

Secure Access Service Edge

Secure Access Service Edge (SASE) is an emerging cybersecurity architecture that provides comprehensive and integrated security services, to protect the network and data in the cloud. SASE combines wide area networking (WAN) and network security services, such as firewalls, intrusion detection and prevention, secure web gateways, and zero-trust network access into a single cloud-based service.

SASE architecture enables organizations to securely connect users and devices to applications, regardless of location, in a more flexible and scalable way. SASE technology operates on a cloud-based platform that provides users with secure access to the network regardless of their location or device type.

SASE provides a holistic approach to security, integrating multiple security functions, such as antivirus, anti-malware, and web filtering into a single, cohesive solution. SASE technology also incorporates identity and access management tools to ensure secure access to applications and data. By consolidating security services into a single, cloud-based platform, SASE technology simplifies security management and reduces the need for complex, hardware-based security solutions.

Popular vendors of SASE technology include Cisco, Zscaler, Palo Alto Networks, and Fortinet. These vendors offer a range of solutions that provide comprehensive and integrated security services, network connectivity, and optimization in a cloud-based platform.

Containerization

Containerization is a technology that allows applications to run in a self-contained environment or container separate from the host operating system. Containers are an efficient and lightweight way to package, distribute, and run software applications, as they encapsulate all the necessary dependencies and libraries required for the application to run.

Containerization can help improve cybersecurity by providing a secure runtime environment that is isolated from the host operating system and by allowing applications to be more easily deployed and scaled. This can help organizations reduce the attack surface of their applications and improve their ability to respond to security incidents.

The most popular containerization technology is Docker, an open source containerization platform that allows developers to build, ship, and run applications in containers. Other popular containerization technologies include Kubernetes, a container orchestration platform, and AWS Fargate, a serverless container platform.

In addition to improving cybersecurity, containerization can help organizations reduce costs by allowing them to run more applications on the same infrastructure and making it easier to deploy and manage applications. However, it is important to note that containerization is not a silver bullet solution for all cybersecurity challenges and must be implemented alongside other security measures.

Artificial Intelligence and Machine Learning

Artificial intelligence (AI) and machine learning (ML) have emerged as powerful technologies that can significantly enhance cybersecurity capabilities. These technologies, such as ChatGPT and Google Bard, have the potential to revolutionize how organizations detect and respond to threats in real time by using advanced algorithms and data analysis techniques.

AI in cybersecurity involves the development of intelligent systems that can simulate human-like thinking and decision-making processes. Natural language processing

(NLP) models like ChatGPT can understand and respond to human-generated text, enabling automated analysis of vast amounts of data, such as security logs, threat intelligence reports, and user communications. ML algorithms, including deep learning models like convolutional neural networks (CNNs) and recurrent neural networks (RNNs), enable computers to learn patterns and features from training data without explicit programming, enabling effective anomaly detection and predictive analytics.

When applied to cybersecurity, AI and ML can automate various processes, augment human capabilities, and enhance the overall effectiveness of cybersecurity defenses. For example, AI algorithms can autonomously monitor network traffic, detect and classify known malware signatures, and identify suspicious behaviors indicative of zero-day attacks. ML models can analyze historical attack data to uncover hidden patterns and create robust predictive models that anticipate and prevent future attacks.

AI-powered cybersecurity systems can also automate repetitive tasks, freeing up security professionals to focus on more strategic activities. Chatbot technologies, such as Google Dialogflow, Amazon Lex, and Microsoft Bot Framework, can provide instant support and guidance to users, help triage security incidents, and provide real-time threat intelligence. This automation enables faster response times, reduces human error, and improves overall incident response efficiency.

However, it is essential to note that AI and ML in cybersecurity are not without challenges. The effectiveness of these technologies relies heavily on the quality and diversity of the data used for training the algorithms. Biased or incomplete training data can lead to inaccurate or discriminatory outcomes. Adversaries are also using AI techniques, known as adversarial AI, to develop sophisticated attacks that can evade traditional defense mechanisms.

This cat-and-mouse game between attackers and defenders requires ongoing research and development to stay ahead of emerging threats.

To use the potential of AI and ML in cybersecurity, organizations need to invest in robust data collection and processing capabilities. They should also prioritize data privacy and security to ensure that sensitive information, such as personally identifiable information (PII), is adequately protected during AI-driven analysis. Regular monitoring, auditing, and fine-tuning of AI algorithms are necessary to maintain optimal performance and adapt to evolving threats.

AI and ML, including technologies like ChatGPT and Google Bard, are transforming the cybersecurity landscape by enabling organizations to detect and respond to threats faster and more accurately. These technologies have the potential to revolutionize how we defend against cyberattacks, but they require careful implementation, ongoing refinement, and ethical considerations to maximize their benefits while mitigating potential risks. As the cybersecurity landscape continues to evolve, AI and ML will play an increasingly critical role in safeguarding organizations from emerging threats.

Blockchain

Blockchain technology has emerged as a transformative innovation with potential applications across various industries, including cybersecurity. By using the fundamental principles of decentralization, immutability, and transparency, blockchain can enhance the security and integrity of digital transactions and data.

In cybersecurity, blockchain can be used to create a tamper-proof ledger of transactions and data, providing an immutable record that cannot be altered or manipulated. This decentralized nature of blockchain eliminates the need for a central authority or intermediary, reducing the risk of single points of failure and enhancing the overall security posture.

One of the key features of blockchain is its ability to ensure data integrity. Each transaction or data entry is cryptographically linked to the previous one, forming a chain of blocks that is continuously verified and validated by a distributed network of participants, known as *nodes*. Any attempt to alter a previous block would require a consensus among the majority of nodes in the network, making it highly resistant to tampering or unauthorized modifications.

In the context of cybersecurity, blockchain can be particularly useful in areas, such as identity management and authentication. Traditional identity management systems often rely on centralized databases that can be vulnerable to data breaches or unauthorized access. By using blockchain, identities can be securely stored and managed in a decentralized manner, providing individuals with greater control over their personal information and reducing the risk of identity theft or impersonation.

Blockchain can also enhance the security of supply chains and digital asset management. By recording each step of the supply chain process on the blockchain, organizations can ensure transparency and traceability, reducing the risk of counterfeit products or unauthorized modifications. Similarly, blockchain-based systems can enable the secure transfer and tracking of digital assets, such as cryptocurrencies or intellectual property, with built-in mechanisms for verifying ownership and preventing unauthorized duplication.

While blockchain technology offers promising benefits for cybersecurity, it is important to consider its limitations. Blockchain is not a silver bullet solution and may not be suitable for all use cases. The scalability and performance of blockchain networks can be challenging, especially when dealing with high transaction volumes or real-time data processing. Additionally, cryptographic algorithms and robust key management practices are essential to ensure the security of blockchain implementations.

Blockchain technology has the potential to revolutionize cybersecurity by providing tamper-proof transaction and data integrity. By taking advantage of blockchain's decentralized and transparent nature, organizations can enhance the security of digital transactions, identity management, supply chains, and digital asset management. However, careful consideration of its limitations and proper implementation practices are necessary to maximize the benefits of blockchain in cybersecurity. As the technology continues to evolve, blockchain is poised to play a significant role in mitigating cyber threats and ensuring the integrity and trustworthiness of digital systems.

Quantum Computing

Quantum computing represents a paradigm shift in computing technology with the potential to disrupt various fields, including cybersecurity. Unlike classical computers, which use bits to process information in binary states of 0s and 1s, quantum computers use *quantum bits*, or *qubits*, which can exist in multiple states simultaneously due to the principles of quantum mechanics.

One of the significant implications of quantum computing for cybersecurity is its potential to break the encryption methods currently used to secure sensitive data. Many encryption algorithms, such as RSA (Rivest-Shamir-Adleman) and ECC (Elliptic Curve Cryptography), rely on the difficulty of factoring large numbers or solving mathematical problems believed to be computationally infeasible for classical computers. However, quantum computers, with their ability to perform complex calculations and exploit quantum algorithms like Shor's algorithm, could potentially solve these problems much more efficiently.

The potential decryption capability of quantum computers poses a significant challenge to the security of encrypted data transmitted over networks and stored in databases. Confidential information that relies on encryption to protect its confidentiality and integrity, such as financial transactions, personal data, and trade secrets, could become vulnerable to unauthorized access or exploitation.

As board members, it is crucial to be aware of the potential implications of quantum computing for cybersecurity. Understanding the potential risks and challenges enables proactive planning and strategizing to mitigate the impact. Here are some key considerations:

- *Post-quantum cryptography*: Board members should be aware of ongoing efforts in the field of post-quantum cryptography focusing on developing encryption algorithms that are resistant to attacks from quantum computers. Collaborating with cybersecurity experts and staying informed about advancements in post-quantum cryptographic standards will be essential in preparing for the quantum era.
- *Risk assessment and encryption life-cycle management*: Organizations must assess their current encryption practices and identify critical systems and data that may be vulnerable to quantum attacks. Implementing robust encryption life-cycle management, including key management and regular encryption algorithm updates, can help mitigate risks associated with quantum computing.
- *Collaboration and partnerships*: Boards should encourage collaboration with industry peers, government agencies, and research institutions to stay informed about the latest developments in quantum computing and their impact on cybersecurity. Engaging with experts and participating in industry initiatives can provide valuable insights and inform decision-making processes.

- *Quantum-safe solutions*: Exploring and investing in quantum-safe solutions is crucial for future-proofing cybersecurity defenses. These solutions aim to provide encryption algorithms and protocols that are resistant to attacks from both classical and quantum computers. Evaluating and adopting quantum-safe solutions when they become available will be vital in maintaining data security in the quantum computing era.
- *Continuous monitoring and adaptation*: Quantum computing is still in its early stages, and the timeline for practical quantum computers remains uncertain. However, board members should ensure that their organization has a proactive approach to cybersecurity, including continuous monitoring of technological advancements, threat intelligence, and risk assessments. This allows organizations to adapt their cybersecurity strategies accordingly as quantum computing progresses.

While quantum computing presents potential challenges for cybersecurity, it also offers opportunities for innovation. Quantum-resistant encryption methods and quantum key distribution protocols are being explored to enhance security in the quantum era. Board members should stay informed, engage with experts, and actively participate in shaping the cybersecurity strategies of their organization to navigate the changing landscape brought about by quantum computing. By doing so, organizations can prepare themselves to tackle future cyber threats effectively and safeguard sensitive data from quantum-enabled attacks.

Cybersecurity Incident: VerticalScope

In 2016, Canadian company VerticalScope suffered a data breach that affected more than 45 million

(continued)

(continued)

user accounts across 1,100 of its online communities, including automotive, sports, and technology forums. The breach was caused by a vulnerability in the company's software, which allowed hackers to gain access to user email addresses, usernames, and hashed passwords.

The attackers used the stolen email addresses and passwords to launch credential-stuffing attacks, where they tried to use the same usernames and passwords on other sites to gain access to additional accounts. While the stolen passwords were hashed, it was discovered that the hashing algorithm used by VerticalScope was weak, which made it easier for attackers to crack the passwords.

The company faced legal action for the breach. In 2018, VerticalScope settled a class-action lawsuit for $2.3 million, which included compensation for affected users and attorneys' fees.

Threat Intelligence

As cyber threats continue to evolve, threat intelligence has become an essential tool for organizations to stay ahead of cybercriminals. Threat intelligence involves the collection, analysis, and dissemination of information about potential cyber threats to help organizations better understand the risks they face and make informed decisions about how to protect themselves. Board members play a critical role in ensuring that their organization has the necessary threat intelligence to mitigate cyber risks effectively. In this section, we will discuss what threat intelligence is, how it can help organizations, and what board members should know about it.

What Is Threat Intelligence?

Threat intelligence is information collected, analyzed, and shared about potential cyber threats. Threat intelligence can come from a variety of sources and can include internal data, open source intelligence, and information shared by other organizations. It is used to identify potential threats, assess their severity and likelihood, and provide insights into how to prevent or respond to them. Threat intelligence can be used to inform security operations, incident response, risk management, and compliance programs.

How Can Threat Intelligence Help Organizations?

Threat intelligence can provide a wide range of benefits to organizations, including the following:

- *Early detection*: Threat intelligence can help organizations detect potential threats early on, allowing them to take proactive measures to mitigate the risks before they become a problem.
- *Risk mitigation*: Threat intelligence can help organizations identify vulnerabilities and weaknesses in their systems and applications, allowing them to take steps to mitigate the risks before they are exploited.
- *Incident response*: Threat intelligence can provide valuable insights into the nature of cyber threats, including the tools, techniques, and procedures used by attackers. This information can help organizations develop effective incident response plans and protocols.
- *Compliance*: Threat intelligence can help organizations identify potential compliance risks and ensure that they are meeting regulatory requirements.

What Should Board Members Know About Threat Intelligence?

Board members play a critical role in ensuring that their organization has the necessary threat intelligence to mitigate cyber risks effectively. Here are some key things that board members should know about threat intelligence:

- *The importance of threat intelligence*: Board members should understand the critical role that threat intelligence plays in identifying and mitigating cyber risks. They should also be aware of the potential consequences of failing to implement a threat intelligence program, including data breaches, reputational damage, and regulatory fines.

- *The different types of threat intelligence*: Board members should be familiar with the different types of threat intelligence, including internal data, open-source intelligence, and information shared by other organizations. They should also understand the strengths and limitations of each type of threat intelligence and how they can be used to inform decision-making.

- *The need for a holistic approach*: Board members should understand that effective threat intelligence requires a holistic approach that involves collecting and analyzing data from a wide range of sources. They should also be aware of the importance of integrating threat intelligence with other security programs, such as incident response, risk management, and compliance.

- *The importance of actionable intelligence*: Board members should understand that threat intelligence is valuable only if it is actionable. They should ensure that their organization has the necessary resources and capabilities to act on the intelligence it receives and that there is a clear process for translating threat intelligence into action.

Threat intelligence is an essential tool for organizations to identify and mitigate cyber risks. Board members play a critical role in ensuring that their organization has the necessary threat intelligence to protect against cyber threats effectively. By understanding the importance of threat intelligence, the different types of threat intelligence, the need for a holistic approach, and the importance of actionable intelligence, board members can help their organization stay ahead of cybercriminals and mitigate the risks they face.

Threat Actors

In today's rapidly evolving digital landscape, it's not just cybercriminals who pose a threat to a company's cybersecurity. A variety of actors can be involved in cyberattacks, ranging from insiders to nation-states. Board members must be aware of these actors and understand their motivations to effectively oversee their company's cybersecurity program.

In this section, we will provide an overview of the key actors involved in cybersecurity, including their motivations and tactics. We will also discuss how board members can work with their management team to develop strategies for protecting against these actors and responding to cyber incidents. By understanding the key actors in cybersecurity, board members can better position their company to mitigate cyber risks and protect valuable data and assets.

Cybersecurity Incident: Code Spaces

In 2014, Code Spaces, a small cloud-based code hosting platform, was the victim of a devastating cyberattack that ultimately led to the company going

(continued)

(continued)

out of business. The attackers gained access to the company's Amazon Web Services (AWS) console and demanded a ransom in exchange for relinquishing control.

When Code Spaces refused to pay the ransom, the attackers began to systematically delete data from the company's servers, including backups, virtual machines, and machine configurations. The attack was so severe that it ultimately resulted in a complete data wipe of Code Spaces' servers, effectively rendering the company's service inoperable.

Code Spaces' board of directors was involved in the aftermath of the attack and decided to shut down the company. In a statement at the time, the company cited the severity of the damage caused by the attack as the reason for its closure, stating that it was impossible to recover from the complete data wipe.

While it's unclear whether the board of directors was directly involved in the incident response or whether they had any prior knowledge of the vulnerability that allowed the attack to occur, the incident highlights the need for companies of all sizes to take cybersecurity seriously and have robust measures in place to prevent, detect, and respond to cyber threats.

External Threat Actors

The following are external threat actors.

State-Sponsored Attackers

State-sponsored attackers, also known as *advanced persistent threats*, are among the most dangerous and sophisticated threat actors in the cybersecurity landscape. These attackers are typically backed by nation-states, and their objective is often to steal sensitive data, disrupt operations, or gain access to critical systems.

State-sponsored attackers have the resources and technical capabilities to launch complex and persistent attacks that can go undetected for months or even years. They often use advanced tactics, techniques, and procedures (TTPs) to gain a foothold in a targeted organization's network, such as social engineering, spear-phishing, and exploiting zero-day vulnerabilities.

Once inside a network, state-sponsored attackers use a variety of techniques to maintain persistence and move laterally to gain access to sensitive data or critical systems. This can include installing backdoors, creating fake user accounts, and using remote access tools to maintain a foothold in the network.

State-sponsored attackers are a particularly concerning threat to organizations because they typically have very specific goals, such as stealing intellectual property, disrupting critical infrastructure, or conducting espionage. They are often able to operate with relative impunity, as they are shielded by their nation-state backers and have access to significant resources, including cutting-edge technology and intelligence.

To defend against state-sponsored attackers, organizations need to be proactive and implement a comprehensive cybersecurity program that includes measures, such as network segmentation, access controls, threat intelligence, and advanced detection and response capabilities. It is also critical to have incident response plans in place to ensure a rapid and effective response to any potential attacks.

Some of the best-known state-sponsored attackers include APT10 (also known as Stone Panda), APT29 (also known as Cozy Bear), and APT33 (also known as Elfin). These groups have been implicated in numerous high-profile attacks, including the theft of intellectual property and sensitive government data.

Hacktivists

Hacktivists are individuals or groups who use hacking as a means to achieve their social or political goals. Their attacks are usually aimed at businesses or organizations they believe are acting against their beliefs, values, or causes.

Hacktivist attacks can include website defacement, distributed denial-of-service (DDoS) attacks, and theft or exposure of sensitive information. They may also use social engineering techniques to gain access to systems, such as phishing emails or social media manipulation.

One of the best-known hacktivist groups is Anonymous, which has carried out numerous attacks on targets, including government organizations, corporations, and individuals. Their actions have ranged from online protests and website defacements to major data breaches.

Board members should be aware of the potential threat posed by hacktivists and understand the motivations behind their attacks. By understanding the social or political issues that may motivate these groups, board members can better anticipate and prepare for potential attacks. Organizations should also have a plan for dealing with hacktivist attacks and minimizing the impact on the business. It is important for board members to work closely with their cybersecurity teams to develop and implement effective security strategies to defend against these types of attacks.

Popular hacktivist groups that have emerged in recent years include LulzSec, AntiSec, and GhostSec.

Cybercriminals

Cybercriminals are individuals or groups who engage in criminal activities in cyberspace. Their primary goal is to make financial gains by exploiting vulnerabilities in computer systems and networks, stealing sensitive data, and disrupting critical infrastructure. Cybercriminals can be individuals or part of a larger criminal organization, and they often use sophisticated techniques to carry out their attacks.

There are various types of cybercriminals, each with specific tactics, techniques, and motivations. For example, some cybercriminals may focus on stealing personal information, such as credit card numbers and bank account details, while others may target businesses for financial gain or to disrupt operations.

One common tactic used by cybercriminals is *phishing*: sending fake emails or messages that appear to be from a legitimate source, such as a bank or a popular e-commerce website. These messages usually contain a link or attachment that, when clicked or opened, can install malware or lead to a fake login page where the victim enters their login credentials.

Another tactic used by cybercriminals is *ransomware*: infecting a victim's computer or network with malware that encrypts all their data, making it inaccessible. The cybercriminal then demands a ransom payment in exchange for the decryption key needed to unlock the data.

Some popular cybercriminal groups include FIN7, Carbanak, and the Lazarus Group, among others. These groups are known for carrying out some of the most sophisticated and large-scale cyberattacks, targeting financial institutions, retailers, and government agencies.

To protect against cybercriminals, companies must implement robust security measures, such as firewalls, antivirus and anti-malware software, intrusion detection and prevention systems, and regular data backups. Additionally, employees should be trained on best practices for cybersecurity, such as not opening suspicious emails or attachments and using strong passwords.

Competitors

Competitors are key threat actors in the cybersecurity land-scape that board members should be aware of. Competitors may seek to gain a competitive advantage through various means, including stealing intellectual property or confiden-tial business information. They may also seek to disrupt or sabotage their competitors' operations, such as by launch-ing DDoS attacks or spreading false information.

Competitor-based cyberattacks can take many forms, such as social engineering attacks targeting employees, sup-ply chain attacks targeting third-party vendors or partners, and cyber espionage to steal trade secrets or other sensitive information. Competitors may also use malware or other hacking tools to gain unauthorized access to their competi-tors' networks or systems.

It is important for board members to be aware of the potential threat posed by competitors and ensure that their company's cybersecurity program includes measures to protect against these types of attacks. These may include implementing strong access controls, regularly monitor-ing networks and systems for suspicious activity, and con-ducting regular vulnerability assessments and penetration testing. In addition, board members should ensure that employees are trained to recognize and report suspicious activity and that their company has a plan for responding to cyber incidents involving competitors.

Terrorists

Terrorists are another key threat actor in the realm of cyber-security. They are individuals or groups who use violence and intimidation for political or ideological reasons. While terrorists have traditionally focused on physical attacks, they have increasingly turned to cyberattacks as a means of achieving their goals.

Terrorist groups may use cyberattacks for a variety of purposes, including disrupting critical infrastructure, stealing sensitive information, and spreading propaganda. They may also use social media and other online platforms to recruit and radicalize individuals.

One example of a terrorist cyberattack is the 2014 Sony Pictures hack, which was attributed to North Korea. The attack was carried out in response to the release of the film *The Interview*, which depicted the assassination of North Korean leader Kim Jong-un. The hackers, who identified themselves as the Guardians of Peace, stole sensitive data and released it to the public, causing significant damage to Sony Pictures.

Board members should be aware of the potential for terrorist cyberattacks and the potential impact on their company's operations and reputation. They should ensure that their cybersecurity programs include measures to protect against these threats, such as monitoring for suspicious activity, implementing strong access controls, and training employees on best practices for cybersecurity hygiene. Additionally, they should stay informed about emerging threats and collaborate with government agencies and other companies in their industry to share information and best practices.

Internal Actors

The following are internal threat actors.

Employees

Internal actors, specifically employees, pose a significant threat to the security of an organization. While most employees are trustworthy and do not intend to harm the company, there are instances where employees may intentionally or unintentionally compromise the organization's cybersecurity.

One of the primary ways in which employees may compromise the organization's cybersecurity is through the misuse of their access privileges. For example, an employee with access to sensitive information may unintentionally click a phishing email or download malware, allowing an attacker to access the company's network. Alternatively, an employee with malicious intent may intentionally steal data or plant malware within the organization's network.

Employees may also inadvertently cause cybersecurity incidents through human error. For instance, an employee may leave a laptop containing sensitive data in a public place or fail to install software updates, leaving the company's systems vulnerable to cyberattacks.

It is essential for organizations to have robust policies and procedures in place to mitigate the risk of internal actors compromising their cybersecurity. This includes ensuring that access privileges are appropriately granted and monitored, providing regular cybersecurity training to employees to raise awareness of common threats and how to avoid them, and implementing strong cybersecurity controls, such as data encryption and multifactor authentication.

Additionally, organizations should have a clear incident response plan in place to swiftly respond to any cybersecurity incidents, including those caused by employees. The incident response plan should include steps to contain the incident, mitigate any damage, and prevent similar incidents from occurring in the future.

Board members should be aware of the risks posed by internal actors and ensure that their organization has robust cybersecurity policies and procedures to minimize these risks. They should also ensure that employees are regularly trained on cybersecurity best practices and that the incident response plan is up to date and tested regularly so the organization can respond swiftly and effectively to any cybersecurity incidents, including those caused by employees.

Contractors

Contractors are another type of insider threat that board members should be aware of. A *contractor* is an individual or organization hired by a company to perform specific services or tasks. Contractors can have access to sensitive company data and systems, making them a potential threat to the company's cybersecurity.

Board members should be aware of two types of contractors: temporary contractors and third-party contractors. Temporary contractors are hired on a short-term basis to perform specific tasks or services, such as IT support or marketing. Third-party contractors, on the other hand, are contracted by a company to provide services or products on an ongoing basis, such as a cloud service provider or a software vendor.

Like employees, contractors can pose a significant insider threat if they are not properly vetted or trained. They may intentionally or unintentionally cause a data breach or leak sensitive information. For example, a third-party contractor could accidentally expose a database of customer information, or an IT contractor could intentionally steal company data for personal gain.

To mitigate the risks posed by contractors, board members should ensure that their company has a comprehensive vendor management program. This program should include a thorough vetting process for contractors, with background checks and reviews of their cybersecurity practices. Additionally, contractors should be required to sign nondisclosure agreements and adhere to the company's cybersecurity policies.

Popular vendors that offer contractor management solutions include SAP Fieldglass, WorkMarket, and Coupa. These solutions help companies manage their contractor workforce, ensure compliance with regulations and policies, and minimize the risk of insider threats.

Third-Party Vendors

Third-party vendors can be a significant source of cybersecurity risk for organizations. Third-party vendors are external entities providing services, products, or access to systems that are critical to an organization's operations. These vendors may include cloud service providers, software vendors, managed service providers, and other service providers.

The risks associated with third-party vendors can range from data breaches and information leaks to service interruptions and legal liability. For example, a vendor may have access to sensitive data, such as PII, and may inadvertently or intentionally disclose or misuse that data.

It is essential for board members to understand the risks associated with third-party vendors and take steps to mitigate those risks. These steps may include conducting due diligence on vendors before entering into contracts, ensuring that vendor contracts include appropriate security and data protection requirements, and conducting regular security audits and assessments of vendors.

Board members should also ensure that their organization has a vendor risk management program to manage third-party vendor risks effectively. This program should include policies and procedures for assessing and managing vendor risks, as well as processes for monitoring and enforcing vendor compliance with security and data protection requirements.

Some popular vendors in the third-party risk management space include RSA Archer, BitSight, and RiskRecon.

These vendors provide tools and platforms to help organizations manage and mitigate the risks associated with their third-party vendors.

Motivations of Threat Actors

Threat actors in cybersecurity can be motivated by a variety of factors, ranging from financial gain to political or personal objectives. Understanding the motivations of these actors is key to developing effective cybersecurity strategies and safeguarding against potential cyberattacks. This section will explore the various motivations of threat actors, including financial gain, political and strategic objectives, ideological beliefs, and personal motivations. By delving deeper into the reasons behind different types of cyberattacks, board members can gain a better understanding of the nature of cyber threats and how to address them effectively.

Financial Gain

Financial gain is one of the primary motivations for threat actors, including cybercriminals and state-sponsored hackers. In the context of cybersecurity, *financial gain* refers to the monetary benefit that threat actors seek to obtain through their attacks. Cybercriminals, for example, may target businesses and individuals to steal sensitive information, such as credit card numbers, bank account information, and personal data, which they can then use or sell on the dark web for financial gain. Similarly, state-sponsored hackers may conduct cyber espionage or theft of intellectual property to support their country's economic or political interests.

In some cases, cybercriminals may use ransomware for financial gain. Ransomware is a type of malware that locks up a victim's computer or files until a ransom is paid.

The attacker will typically demand payment in a crypto-currency, such as Bitcoin, to make it difficult to track the money trail.

Board members should understand that the motivation of financial gain can make their company an attractive target for cyberattacks. They should ensure that their company takes appropriate measures to secure sensitive data, including implementing access controls, encrypting data, and regularly backing up important information. It is also important for board members to be aware of the financial impact of a cyberattack, including the potential costs of a breach, such as loss of business, reputational damage, and legal fees.

Some of the most notable cyberattacks motivated by financial gain include the 2013 Target data breach, which resulted in the theft of 40 million credit card numbers, and the 2017 WannaCry ransomware attack, which impacted more than 200,000 computers in 150 countries and resulted in losses of up to $4 billion.

Popular cybersecurity companies that offer solutions to protect against financial gain include CrowdStrike, FireEye, and Palo Alto Networks.

Political and Strategic Objectives

Political and strategic objectives are significant motivations for threat actors involved in cybersecurity attacks. These actors can include state-sponsored hackers, hacktivists, and other groups seeking to advance political or strategic goals through cyberattacks.

The objectives of these threat actors can vary widely depending on the group involved. Some state-sponsored hackers, for example, may try to steal military or government secrets from foreign countries to gain a strategic advantage. Other groups may aim to disrupt critical infrastructure or other key systems to cause chaos and harm to a target country or organization.

In addition to state-sponsored hackers, hacktivist groups may use cyberattacks to advance political or social causes. These groups may target organizations or individuals that they perceive as working against their objectives or see as vulnerable to attack.

Board members need to be aware of the political and strategic motivations of threat actors to better understand the potential risks facing their organization. By understanding the objectives of these groups, board members can better assess the potential impact of an attack and take appropriate steps to protect their company's critical assets.

It is important to note that political and strategic objectives are not always the only motivations for cyberattacks. Other motivations, such as financial gain, ideological beliefs, and personal motivations, may also come into play, and board members need to be aware of all potential motivations to develop a comprehensive cybersecurity strategy.

Ideological Beliefs

Threat actors can be motivated by ideological beliefs, including religious, social, or political views. Sometimes these motivations may be linked to extremist or terrorist organizations.

For example, a threat actor may launch a cyberattack on a company to steal sensitive information or disrupt operations to advance their extremist ideology. The threat actor may attack companies they view as opposing their beliefs or to generate publicity and spread their message.

Board members should be aware of the potential for threat actors to be motivated by ideological beliefs and the potential impact this can have on their company. This may include an increased risk of targeted attacks, reputational damage, and financial loss. Understanding the motivations and tactics of these threat actors can help the company better prepare for and respond to potential attacks.

The board needs to work closely with the company's security and risk management teams to identify potential threats, assess risk and impact, and develop a plan for mitigating these risks. This may include implementing security controls, conducting regular security assessments, and ensuring that employees are trained on best practices for cybersecurity. By taking these steps, the company can better protect against cyberattacks motivated by ideological beliefs and maintain the integrity of its business operations.

Personal Motivations

Personal motivations can also be a driving factor for threat actors in carrying out cyberattacks. Unlike other motivations, personal motivations are driven not by external factors, such as financial or political gain but rather by internal factors.

The following are some personal motivations that can drive threat actors to launch cyberattacks:

- *Revenge*: Disgruntled or former employees may seek revenge against their employers for perceived grievances, leading them to steal sensitive information or disrupt business operations.
- *Thrill-seeking*: Some individuals may be motivated to launch cyberattacks simply for the thrill of it. They may enjoy the challenge of breaking into a secure network or causing damage to systems.
- *Notoriety*: Individuals may launch cyberattacks to gain notoriety within hacker communities or prove their technical abilities.
- *Extortion*: Some threat actors may carry out attacks to extort money or other resources from their victims. For

example, they may threaten to leak sensitive information or disrupt operations unless a ransom is paid.

Board members should be aware of the potential for personal motivations to drive cyberattacks, as these can be difficult to predict and mitigate. Organizations can mitigate this risk by implementing effective employee screening and monitoring programs, ensuring that access controls are in place, and educating employees about the risks of engaging in malicious activities.

In addition, companies can work to create a positive workplace culture and foster strong employee engagement to reduce the likelihood of employees being motivated by personal factors to engage in malicious cyber activities.

Tactics, Techniques, and Procedures

Tactics, techniques, and procedures refer to threat actors' methods to achieve their goals. TTPs are often specific to the type of threat actor and their motivations. For example, state-sponsored attackers may have different TTPs than hacktivists or cybercriminals. Understanding the TTPs used by threat actors can help organizations identify and prevent attacks and respond more effectively if a breach occurs. By analyzing TTPs, security professionals can identify patterns and indicators of compromise and use that information to develop better defenses against cyber threats.

Examples of TTPs Used by Different Threat Actors

Threat actors use tactics, techniques, and procedures to achieve their objectives. Understanding the TTPs different threat actors use is essential for organizations to strengthen their cybersecurity defenses. Here are some examples of TTPs used by different threat actors:

- *State-sponsored actors*: These actors often have significant resources and use sophisticated TTPs to achieve their objectives. They use a variety of tactics, including spear phishing, watering hole attacks, and supply chain attacks. They also use advanced persistent threats to remain undetected for long periods. For example, the Russian APT group Fancy Bear used spear-phishing emails to access the Democratic National Committee's servers during the 2016 U.S. presidential election.

- *Cybercriminals*: Cybercriminals are motivated by financial gain and use TTPs to steal data, extort money, and commit other cybercrimes. Common TTPs cybercriminals use include ransomware attacks, business email compromise (BEC), and social engineering attacks. For example, the ransomware group REvil used a zero-day exploit to attack Kaseya's VSA software in July 2021, resulting in one of the largest ransomware attacks in history.

- *Hacktivists*: Hacktivists are motivated by political or social causes and use TTPs to achieve their objectives. They often use DDoS attacks, website defacements, and data leaks to promote their causes. For example, the hacktivist group Anonymous launched a DDoS attack against PayPal in 2010 in response to the company's decision to stop processing donations to WikiLeaks.

- *Competitors*: Competitors may use TTPs to gain a competitive advantage or steal valuable data. They may use social engineering attacks, spear phishing, or supply chain attacks to achieve their objectives. For example, in 2016, Uber was accused of using TTPs to steal trade secrets from its competitor, Waymo.

- *Insiders*: Insiders, such as employees, contractors, and third-party vendors, may use TTPs to steal data, sabotage systems, or commit other cybercrimes. They may use social engineering attacks, phishing, or other methods to access sensitive data. For example, in 2019, a former employee of Capital One Bank used a misconfigured firewall to gain access to customer data and was charged with data theft.

In conclusion, understanding the TTPs used by different threat actors is essential for organizations to develop effective cybersecurity defenses. Threat actors use a range of tactics, from simple social engineering attacks to sophisticated APTs. By understanding the TTPs used by threat actors, organizations can implement appropriate controls to protect against cyber threats.

MITRE ATT&CK Framework

The MITRE ATT&CK framework is a comprehensive knowledge base of cyber threats, tactics, and techniques threat actors use. It is a globally recognized cyber threat intelligence tool used by various organizations, including government agencies, private businesses, and cybersecurity vendors. The framework provides a common language for understanding and communicating cybersecurity threats, which makes it easier to share information and collaborate with other organizations.

As a board member, it is important to understand the MITRE ATT&CK framework and its role in threat intelligence. By familiarizing themselves with this framework, board members can better understand their organization's cybersecurity risks and help guide the company's cybersecurity strategy.

The MITRE ATT&CK framework breaks down cyber threats into tactics and techniques threat actors use to gain unauthorized access, move laterally within an organization's network, and achieve their objectives. The framework includes several categories of tactics and techniques, including initial access, execution, persistence, and exfiltration.

Organizations can better identify and prioritize cyber-security risks by understanding threat actors' tactics and techniques. This information can also be used to develop more effective security controls, such as intrusion detection and prevention systems, endpoint protection, and network segmentation.

The MITRE ATT&CK framework provides a common language for sharing threat intelligence between organizations. Using this framework, board members can communicate more effectively with other organizations about threat actors' specific tactics and techniques. This can help organizations collaborate more effectively and respond quickly to emerging threats.

The MITRE ATT&CK framework is important for understanding and communicating cybersecurity threats. As a board member, being familiar with this framework and understanding how it can guide a company's cybersecurity strategy is important. Using the MITRE ATT&CK framework, organizations can better identify and prioritize cyber-security risks, develop more effective security controls, and collaborate more effectively with other organizations.

Board members can learn more about the MITRE ATT&CK framework through a variety of sources, including the following:

- *MITRE website*: The MITRE ATT&CK framework is free on the MITRE website (www.mitre.org), along with a wealth of information on its development and use.
- *Cybersecurity vendors*: Many cybersecurity vendors incorporate the MITRE ATT&CK framework into their products and services, and they may offer educational materials to help customers understand and implement the framework.
- *Cybersecurity industry events*: Board members can attend cybersecurity industry events, such as conferences and

workshops, where the MITRE ATT&CK framework is often discussed.

- *Cybersecurity consultants*: Board members can engage the services of cybersecurity consultants who are knowledgeable about the MITRE ATT&CK framework and can provide guidance on how to implement it within their organization.
- *Online training courses*: Various online training courses cover the MITRE ATT&CK framework and its implementation. These courses can be self-paced and are often available for free or for a fee.

Chapter 2 Summary

This chapter provided a comprehensive exploration of the fundamental concepts and principles that underpin cybersecurity. We started with the CIA framework, a cornerstone of cybersecurity that outlines the three main objectives of any robust security strategy. This framework serves as a lens through which board members can view and evaluate the effectiveness of their organization's cybersecurity measures.

We then delved into key cybersecurity concepts and terminology, providing board members with the necessary vocabulary to understand and discuss cybersecurity issues effectively. This was followed by an overview of common cyber threats and risks faced by companies today, equipping board members with the knowledge to identify potential threats and understand their potential impact.

Recognizing the dynamic nature of the cyber landscape, we discussed emerging threats and the latest technologies and defense strategies that can be employed to mitigate these threats. This understanding is vital for board members to make informed decisions about their organization's cybersecurity investments.

The chapter also covered the importance of threat intelligence in providing actionable insights about the current threat landscape, enabling companies to proactively defend against potential cyberattacks. We explored the various threat actors in the cyber landscape and their capabilities and tactics, helping board members assess the level of risk their organization faces. We also introduced the MITRE ATT&CK framework, a globally accessible knowledge base of adversary tactics and techniques. This framework can be a valuable tool for board members to understand the various tactics, techniques, and procedures that threat actors use, enabling them to better evaluate their organization's defenses.

This chapter equipped board members with a solid understanding of the basics of cybersecurity, enabling them to play a more active and effective role in their organization's cybersecurity governance. By understanding these fundamentals, board members can help protect their organization from the ever-present threat of cyberattacks and ensure its long-term success in the digital age.

Chapter 3
Legal and Regulatory Landscape

In today's rapidly evolving digital landscape, cybersecurity has become a critical concern for businesses of all sizes. Small and medium-sized businesses face a complex legal and regulatory environment that governs cybersecurity practices. It is crucial for board members to have a comprehensive understanding of this landscape and ensure that their company complies with the latest cybersecurity regulations. This chapter aims to provide a detailed overview of the legal and regulatory framework surrounding cybersecurity, including the relevant laws, regulations, and industry standards that impact SMBs.

Governments worldwide have recognized the importance of cybersecurity and have implemented regulations to enhance data protection, privacy, and overall security. In the United States, the Federal Trade Commission (FTC) has been granted broad authority to regulate and enforce cybersecurity measures. Additionally, individual states have established laws and regulations regarding data breach notifications and safeguarding personal information. Across the European Union, the General Data Protection Regulation (GDPR) has brought significant changes to how companies handle and protect personal data, placing a strong emphasis on privacy and accountability.

Compliance with these legal and regulatory requirements is essential for SMBs to protect their customers' data, maintain their reputation, and mitigate the risk of penalties and legal liability. Failure to comply can result in severe consequences, both financially and reputationally. Therefore, it is crucial for board members to be well versed in the relevant cybersecurity regulations and laws that apply to their organization's operations.

In addition to legal requirements, industry standards play a vital role in cybersecurity governance. Standards such as the Payment Card Industry Data Security Standard (PCI DSS) and the National Institute of Standards and Technology (NIST) Cybersecurity Framework provide guidelines and best practices for organizations to protect their systems, data, and sensitive information. Board members should be familiar with these industry standards and ensure that their company aligns its cybersecurity practices accordingly.

Throughout this chapter, we will delve into the specifics of cybersecurity regulations, laws, and industry standards that board members need to understand. We will explore topics such as federal and state regulations in the United States, European Union regulations, industry standards, compliance requirements, and individual director liability. By gaining a comprehensive understanding of the legal and regulatory landscape, board members can effectively navigate the complexities of cybersecurity governance and ensure that their organization remains secure and compliant.

Cybersecurity Incident: Morgan Stanley

In 2016, Morgan Stanley suffered a data breach that exposed sensitive customer data, including names, addresses, account numbers, and investment information, for more than 350,000 clients. The data was briefly published on the Internet, and the company quickly worked to remove it and notify affected customers.

The breach was traced back to an insider threat: a financial advisor at the company who was allegedly trying to sell the data on the dark web. The advisor was later fired and arrested.

Morgan Stanley's board of directors was involved in the response to the breach, as board members were ultimately responsible for overseeing the company's cybersecurity program and ensuring that appropriate measures were in place to prevent such incidents. The board likely reviewed the incident and worked with management to investigate the root cause, implement remediation measures, and ensure that similar incidents do not occur in the future.

The incident highlighted the importance of having strong insider threat mitigation programs in place, as well as the need for ongoing monitoring and risk assessments to identify and prevent potential data breaches. The board likely took steps to review and enhance the company's cybersecurity program following the breach to prevent future incidents and protect both the company and its customers.

Overview of Relevant Cybersecurity Regulations and Laws

This section will provide an overview of cybersecurity regulations and laws that impact SMBs. It's essential for board members to have a good understanding of these regulations and laws, as failure to comply can lead to significant financial and reputational damage and legal liability.

Federal Regulations in the United States

The following are regulations in the United States.

The Federal Trade Commission Act

The Federal Trade Commission (FTC) Act is a U.S. federal law that empowers the FTC to regulate various unfair or deceptive business practices. This includes rules related to data privacy and cybersecurity.

The FTC has taken a particularly active role in regulating cybersecurity practices and has been involved in some high-profile cybersecurity enforcement actions. As a result, it is essential for boards of directors to be familiar with the FTC Act and its potential implications for their company.

Under the FTC Act, companies that collect and store personal information must take reasonable measures to secure that information. Companies must implement appropriate administrative, technical, and physical safeguards to protect against unauthorized access, use, or disclosure of personal information.

The FTC has published several guidelines and resources to help companies comply with the FTC Act's requirements. Boards of directors should ensure that their company has adequate resources to address these guidelines and should regularly review and assess their cybersecurity practices.

It is important to note that failure to comply with the FTC Act's requirements can result in significant penalties and fines. Additionally, individual board members may be personally liable for their company's failure to comply with the FTC Act if they were aware of the noncompliant practices and failed to take appropriate action to address them. Therefore, board members should take an active role in overseeing their company's cybersecurity practices and ensuring compliance with the FTC Act.

In recent years, the FTC has taken action against several companies for violations related to cybersecurity. One high-profile example is the FTC's action against Uber in 2017. The FTC alleged that Uber had failed to secure its software reasonably and had not adequately protected consumers' sensitive personal information. The FTC also alleged that Uber had misrepresented the extent to which it monitored access to consumer data by its employees. The FTC ultimately settled with Uber, requiring the company to implement a comprehensive privacy program and undergo third-party audits for the next 20 years.

In 2019, the FTC settled with Equifax for a data breach that exposed the personal information of more than 147 million people. The FTC alleged that Equifax had failed to implement reasonable security measures, such as patching known vulnerabilities in its systems. The settlement required Equifax to pay up to $425 million in consumer restitution and provide enhanced data security measures.

In terms of the involvement of the board of directors, it is important for boards to ensure that their companies are implementing reasonable cybersecurity measures to protect sensitive information. This includes conducting regular risk assessments, implementing appropriate policies and procedures, and ensuring that all employees and third-party vendors know and follow cybersecurity best practices.

Boards should also ensure that they receive regular reports on the state of their company's cybersecurity program and any incidents or breaches that may have occurred. If a company experiences a cybersecurity incident or is facing an FTC investigation, the board should take an active role in overseeing the response and ensuring that the company is taking appropriate steps to address the issue and prevent it from happening again.

The FTC Act is an important tool for holding companies accountable for their cybersecurity practices, and boards have an important role in ensuring that their companies comply with the law and protect consumer data.

The Gramm-Leach-Bliley Act

The Gramm-Leach-Bliley Act (GLBA) is a federal law regulating how financial institutions handle sensitive customer information, including personally identifiable financial information. The GLBA has significant implications for cybersecurity because it mandates that financial institutions implement appropriate safeguards to protect customer data.

In cybersecurity, the GLBA requires that financial institutions establish and maintain a comprehensive security program to protect the confidentiality and integrity of customers' information. This security program should be commensurate with the size and complexity of the financial institution, the nature and scope of its activities, and the sensitivity of the customer information it handles.

The security program should include administrative, technical, and physical safeguards to ensure customer information security, confidentiality, and integrity. These safeguards should include, but not be limited to, the following:

- *Employee training and management*: Financial institutions should train their employees to handle customer information securely and have processes to manage and oversee employee compliance.

- *Information systems*: Financial institutions should develop, implement, and maintain secure information systems to protect customer information from unauthorized access, use, disclosure, and destruction.
- *Access controls*: Financial institutions should restrict access to customer information to only those employees who have a business need for the information and should have processes to manage and oversee employee access.
- *Physical safeguards*: Financial institutions should have physical security measures, such as access controls, to protect against unauthorized access to customer information.
- *Incident response*: Financial institutions should have a process to respond to cybersecurity incidents and data breaches, including notifying customers and authorities as required by law.

Board members of financial institutions should be aware of their obligations under the GLBA and ensure that their organization has appropriate cybersecurity policies and procedures to comply with the law. Board members should also ensure that their organization regularly tests and updates its cybersecurity programs to stay current with evolving threats and best practices.

One of the best-known violations of GLBA occurred in 2016 when Morgan Stanley was fined $1 million by the Securities and Exchange Commission (SEC) for failing to protect customer data. The SEC found that Morgan Stanley had failed to implement adequate policies and procedures to protect customer data and properly monitor employee access to customer data.

In terms of the involvement of the board of directors, it is likely that the board was at least partially responsible for the violation of GLBA in the Morgan Stanley case. The board has a responsibility to oversee the company's cybersecurity program and ensure that the company is in compliance with all applicable laws and regulations. If the board had not adequately fulfilled its oversight duties, it could be held accountable for the company's failure to comply with GLBA.

The Health Insurance Portability and Accountability Act

The Health Insurance Portability and Accountability Act (HIPAA) is a U.S. law that sets standards for protecting sensitive patient health information, including electronic health records (EHRs). As a board member, it is important to understand the requirements of HIPAA to ensure that the organization complies with and adequately protects patient health information from unauthorized access or disclosure.

HIPAA includes several key provisions related to cyber-security, such as the following:

- *Security Rule*: HIPAA's Security Rule requires covered entities and business associates to implement administrative, physical, and technical safeguards to protect electronically protected health information (ePHI) from unauthorized access, use, or disclosure.
- *Breach Notification Rule*: HIPAA's Breach Notification Rule requires covered entities and business associates to notify affected individuals, the Department of Health and Human Services (HHS), and, in some cases, the media if there is a breach of unsecured ePHI.
- *Privacy Rule*: HIPAA's Privacy Rule sets standards for protecting the privacy of individuals' health information, including requirements for obtaining individual authorization before using or disclosing protected health information (PHI).

Board members should ensure that their organization has a comprehensive HIPAA compliance program, including policies and procedures to protect ePHI, regular risk assessments, training for employees and contractors, and ongoing monitoring and auditing of security controls. Additionally, board members should ensure that their organization has an incident response plan to respond to potential data breaches, including notifying affected individuals and government agencies as required by HIPAA.

There have been several high-profile HIPAA violations related to cybersecurity over the years. One example is the 2015 data breach at UCLA Health, which affected 4.5 million patients. The breach was caused by a cyberattack that exploited a vulnerability in an IT system. The attackers were able to gain access to sensitive data such as patient names, birth dates, Social Security numbers, and medical information.

In the aftermath of the breach, it was discovered that UCLA Health had failed to implement adequate cybersecurity measures and had not properly trained employees on how to handle sensitive data. The breach resulted in a $7.5 million settlement with the HHS, which oversees HIPAA compliance.

Another example is the 2015 breach at health insurer Anthem, which affected nearly 80 million customers. The breach was caused by a cyberattack that exploited a vulnerability in an IT system and resulted in the theft of sensitive information such as names, dates of birth, Social Security numbers, and medical ID numbers.

In the aftermath of the breach, it was discovered that Anthem had failed to implement adequate cybersecurity measures and had not properly trained employees on how to handle sensitive data. The breach resulted in a $16 million settlement with the HHS.

In both of these cases, the boards of directors of UCLA Health and Anthem were involved in responding to the breaches and were responsible for ensuring that the companies implemented adequate cybersecurity measures and complied with HIPAA regulations. The breaches resulted in significant financial and reputational damage for both companies and underscored the importance of effective cybersecurity governance at the board level.

Cybersecurity Incident: Cottage Health System

In 2015, Cottage Health System, a small healthcare provider in California, suffered a data breach that exposed the personal and medical information of more than 50,000 patients. The breach was caused by a vulnerability in the company's server software that allowed hackers to gain access to patient records.

The data exposed in the breach included patient names, addresses, dates of birth, Social Security numbers, and medical information, such as diagnoses and treatment information. The breach was discovered when some affected patients reported identity theft and fraudulent credit card charges.

Cottage Health System's board of directors was involved in the aftermath of the attack, and the company faced legal action for the breach. In 2018, the company settled a class-action lawsuit for $4.1 million, which included compensation for affected patients and attorneys' fees.

Cybersecurity Incident: Anthem

In February 2015, Anthem, Inc., one of the largest health insurers in the United States, suffered a

(continued)

(continued)

data breach that affected approximately 80 million customers and employees. The breach involved unauthorized access to a database containing personal information, including names, Social Security numbers, birthdates, addresses, and employment information.

As a result of the breach, Anthem's board of directors had to deal with public scrutiny and potential legal repercussions. The company faced lawsuits, regulatory investigations, and fines, and it had to offer free credit monitoring and identity theft protection to affected individuals. The board also had to communicate with investors and other stakeholders about the incident and the company's response. The breach prompted the board to take a closer look at the company's cybersecurity posture, leading to increasing the investment in cybersecurity initiatives and hiring a chief information security officer.

State Regulations in the United States

The following are state regulations in the United States.

Data Breach Notification Laws

Data breach incidents have become common in today's digital landscape, posing significant risks to businesses and their stakeholders. In response to these risks, governments worldwide have enacted data breach notification laws to protect individuals' privacy and promote transparency in the event of a breach. As a board member, understanding the legal obligations imposed by data breach notification laws is crucial for effective cybersecurity governance and risk management.

Data breach notification laws vary from jurisdiction to jurisdiction, with both federal and state regulations playing a role in the United States. These laws typically require companies to notify individuals whose personal information has been compromised in a data breach. While the specific requirements may differ, certain general obligations exist universally.

First, companies are generally obligated to promptly notify affected individuals once a breach is discovered. The notification should include essential details, such as the nature of the information exposed, the potential risks to individuals, and recommended steps for those individuals to protect themselves. Timeliness is critical in this process, with notification typically expected within a specific timeframe, such as 30 to 60 days from the identification of the breach.

Board members must be aware of the data breach notification laws applicable to their organization, considering both federal requirements and any specific regulations within the states in which they operate. Understanding the nuances and variations in these laws is essential to ensure compliance and avoid potential penalties or legal repercussions. Collaborating with legal counsel and cybersecurity professionals can help boards navigate these complexities effectively.

It is crucial for board members to work closely with management to establish clear and comprehensive breach response protocols that align with legal requirements. These protocols should outline the steps to be taken in the event of a breach, including internal investigation, containment measures, and notification processes. Board members should review and approve these protocols, ensuring that they address all relevant legal obligations and industry best practices.

In addition to the legal implications, data breach notification laws carry significant reputational and financial risks for companies. Failing to comply with notification requirements can lead to severe consequences, such as financial penalties, legal liabilities, and damage to the organization's reputation and customer trust. Board members must appreciate the potential ramifications of noncompliance and prioritize the development of robust policies and procedures to meet these obligations.

Board members should also recognize the importance of swift and effective responses in the event of a data breach. A well-prepared incident response plan, aligned with breach notification laws, can help minimize the impact on affected individuals and mitigate potential legal and reputational risks. Regular testing and updating of the incident response plan are critical to ensure its effectiveness and readiness.

By prioritizing compliance with data breach notification laws, board members demonstrate their commitment to safeguarding individual privacy and protecting the organization's interests. Staying informed about changes in the legal landscape and collaborating with experts in the field will enable boards to proactively address potential risks and enhance their overall cybersecurity governance framework.

As cybersecurity threats evolve, board members must remain vigilant, adapting their strategies and practices to effectively manage data breach risks. By understanding data breach notification laws and fulfilling their responsibilities in this area, board members can contribute to a robust cybersecurity posture and uphold stakeholder trust in the face of ever-evolving cyber threats.

California Consumer Privacy Act

The California Consumer Privacy Act (CCPA) provides California residents with certain rights regarding their personal information. It requires companies to disclose what personal information they collect, how it is used, and whom it is shared with. The law also gives consumers the right to request that their personal data be deleted and to opt out of selling their personal information.

From a cybersecurity perspective, the CCPA requires companies to implement reasonable security measures to protect personal information from unauthorized access, disclosure, or destruction. The law also requires companies to implement reasonable procedures to detect, prevent, and respond to security incidents that involve personal information.

For boards of directors, it is essential to be aware of the CCPA's requirements and ensure that their companies comply with the law. This may involve overseeing the implementation of appropriate security measures, ensuring that the company has appropriate incident response procedures in place, and providing appropriate training to employees who handle personal information. Additionally, boards should consider whether their companies are collecting and sharing personal data in compliance with the CCPA and ensure that their companies are prepared to respond to consumer requests for access, deletion, and opt-out of the sale of personal information.

The best-known violation of the CCPA so far was the data breach that occurred at the software company Zynga in 2019. The breach affected more than 200 million users, exposing data including names, email addresses, phone numbers, login IDs, and passwords. While the breach occurred before the CCPA went into effect, the California Attorney General's office opened an investigation to determine if Zynga was in violation of the new law.

Another notable example is the data breach at Capital One in 2019. The breach affected approximately 106 million individuals and involved the theft of personal information including names, addresses, phone numbers, email addresses, and credit scores. The breach was the result of a misconfigured firewall and was attributed to a former

Amazon Web Services employee. Capital One was subsequently fined $80 million for its failure to implement reasonable cybersecurity measures to protect personal information, in violation of the CCPA.

European Union Regulations

The following are European Union regulations.

General Data Protection Regulation

The GDPR is a comprehensive privacy and data protection law enacted by the European Union (EU) in 2018. Although it is an EU law, it has significant implications for businesses outside of the EU, including those based in the United States, that process the personal data of EU citizens.

If a U.S.-based company processes the personal data of EU citizens, it must comply with the GDPR's requirements. The GDPR requires companies to obtain explicit consent from individuals to process their personal data and to provide individuals with certain rights related to their personal data, such as the right to access, rectify, and erase that data.

The GDPR also requires companies to implement appropriate technical and organizational measures to ensure the security of personal data, including efforts to prevent unauthorized access, disclosure, or alteration of that data. In the event of a data breach, companies are required to report the violation to the relevant supervisory authority within 72 hours of becoming aware of it and notify affected individuals if the breach is likely to result in a high risk to their rights and freedoms.

Board members should be aware of the GDPR's requirements and take steps to ensure compliance. This may include appointing a data protection officer, implementing appropriate data security measures, and ensuring that the company's data processing activities are transparent and compliant with the GDPR's requirements.

One of the biggest and best-known violations of the GDPR was the Cambridge Analytica scandal that occurred in 2018. Cambridge Analytica, a political consulting firm, obtained the personal data of millions of Facebook users without their consent and used the information to influence political campaigns, including the U.S. presidential election in 2016. The data was harvested through a personality quiz app created by a third-party developer that was able to collect not only the data of people who took the quiz but also the data of their Facebook friends.

The violation of the GDPR occurred because the data of EU citizens was involved and the data was transferred to a third country (the United States) without proper safeguards. The scandal brought significant public attention to the issue of data privacy and led to increased scrutiny and regulation of social media companies.

In terms of the involvement of the board of directors, there was significant criticism of Facebook's leadership and their handling of the situation. Some argued that the board had not done enough to oversee the company's data protection policies and prevent such a breach from occurring. Facebook CEO Mark Zuckerberg testified before the U.S. Congress and the European Parliament and faced questions from regulators and the public about the company's role in the scandal.

Network and Information Security Directive

The Network and Information Security (NIS) Directive is the first piece of EU-wide cybersecurity legislation. The directive came into effect in 2016 with the goal of enhancing cybersecurity across EU member states. The NIS Directive has a broader scope than the GDPR as it covers all sectors that are vital for the economy and society and also relies heavily on digital infrastructure.

If a U.S.-based board of directors oversees an organization that provides digital services in the EU, such as online marketplaces, search engines, or cloud computing services, it needs to comply with the NIS Directive's requirements. The directive demands that operators of essential services and digital service providers take appropriate security measures and notify the relevant national authority about serious incidents.

Just like the GDPR, the NIS Directive requires organizations to implement appropriate technical and organizational measures to ensure a high level of security of network and information systems. These measures should prevent and minimize the impact of security incidents to ensure service continuity. If a security incident occurs, organizations are obliged to report it to the relevant national authority without undue delay.

Board members should be aware of the NIS Directive's requirements and make certain their organization adheres to them. This can include appointing a dedicated team or individual to handle cybersecurity, implementing robust cybersecurity measures, and ensuring that the organization's network and information system management is transparent and compliant with the NIS Directive's requirements.

A notable example of a security incident that would fall under the purview of the NIS Directive is the 2017 WannaCry ransomware attack. The attack affected hundreds of thousands of computers worldwide, including many in the EU, across various sectors. It notably impacted the National Health Service (NHS) in the UK, causing significant disruption to healthcare services. The malware encrypted data on infected systems and demanded a ransom to decrypt it.

The incident highlighted the importance of maintaining up-to-date systems and having effective incident response plans in place. The subsequent investigation led to the discovery that many of the affected systems were running outdated software, making them vulnerable to the exploit used by the WannaCry ransomware.

In terms of the role of the board of directors, the WannaCry incident underscored the need for boards to take an active role in overseeing their organizations' cybersecurity efforts. Ensuring the implementation of proper security measures, including regular software updates and comprehensive incident response plans, should be a priority for boards to prevent similar incidents in the future.

ePrivacy Directive

The ePrivacy Directive, also known as the Cookie Law, is a piece of EU legislation that focuses on the protection of privacy in the electronic communications sector. Enacted in 2002 and updated in 2009, the ePrivacy Directive complements the general data protection framework established by the GDPR.

If a U.S.-based board of directors oversees an organization that provides electronic communications services in the EU or utilizes such services to process personal data, it needs to comply with the ePrivacy Directive's requirements. Key aspects of the ePrivacy Directive include confidentiality of communications, protection of personal data in the context of electronic communications, and rules about cookies and similar tracking technologies.

The ePrivacy Directive requires organizations to obtain informed consent from users before storing or accessing information on their devices, such as cookies. This is where the common website pop-up asking for cookie consent originates. The Directive also sets rules on unsolicited communications for marketing purposes, which typically take the form of email spam.

Board members should be aware of the ePrivacy Directive's requirements and take steps to ensure that their organization complies. This could include implementing clear and accessible cookie consent mechanisms on company websites, maintaining confidentiality of user communications, and ensuring that any direct marketing activities abide by the rules set out in the ePrivacy Directive.

One significant incident that highlights the implications of the ePrivacy Directive is the Planet49 case. Planet49 GmbH, a German online gaming company, was taken to court for its use of a preselected check box to obtain consent from users to place cookies on their devices for advertising purposes. The Court of Justice of the European Union ruled in 2019 that preselected check boxes do not constitute valid consent under the ePrivacy Directive, setting a precedent for how consent should be obtained for cookies.

The case underscores the importance of the board's role in ensuring proper understanding and implementation of the requirements under the ePrivacy Directive. The board of directors must ensure that the organization has robust mechanisms in place to obtain informed, explicit consent from users before storing or accessing information on their devices, in line with the requirements of the ePrivacy Directive. This is crucial not only for compliance with the law but also for maintaining trust and transparency with users.

Industry Standards

The following are industry standards.

Payment Card Industry Data Security Standard

Payment Card Industry Data Security Standard (PCI DSS) is a set of security standards that govern the processing, storing, and transmission of cardholder data for all entities that accept credit card payments. The Payment Card Industry Security Standards Council (PCI SSC) maintains the standard that major credit card companies formed to establish consistent data security measures across the industry.

For a board of directors, it is important to understand that PCI DSS compliance is a legal requirement and failure to comply can result in significant penalties, including fines and even loss of the ability to process credit card payments. Compliance with PCI DSS involves implementing various technical and operational controls, such as firewalls, encryption, access controls, and regular testing and monitoring.

Board members should ensure that the company has established and maintains the necessary security controls to protect cardholder data and regularly monitors its compliance with the standard. This includes understanding the company's scope of compliance, identifying vulnerabilities, and ensuring that corrective actions are taken promptly. Board members should also ensure that the company has adequate resources and expertise to achieve and maintain compliance and is prepared to respond to any security incidents.

One of the best-known violations of PCI DSS was the Target breach in 2013, where hackers stole the credit and debit card information of 40 million customers, as well as the personal information of 70 million customers. The breach was the result of a vulnerability in Target's payment system that allowed hackers to gain access to the system and steal the data. The breach resulted in an $18.5 million settlement with Mastercard and a $19 million settlement with Visa.

Another significant violation of PCI DSS was the 2017 Equifax data breach, where hackers gained access to the personal information of approximately 143 million customers, including names, addresses, birth dates, and Social Security numbers. The breach was the result of a vulnerability in Equifax's web application software, which the company failed to patch in a timely manner. The breach resulted in a $575 million settlement with the FTC, the

Consumer Financial Protection Bureau, and 50 U.S. states and territories.

In both of these cases, the involvement of the board of directors was significant. In the Target breach, the board was criticized for not prioritizing cybersecurity and failing to take action to address the company's vulnerabilities. In the Equifax breach, the board was criticized for failing to ensure that the company had adequate security measures in place and waiting too long to disclose the breach to customers and the public. As a result, both companies suffered significant financial and reputational damage, highlighting the importance of board involvement in ensuring compliance with PCI DSS and other cybersecurity regulations.

National Institute of Standards and Technology

The National Institute of Standards and Technology (NIST) Cybersecurity Framework (CSF) is a widely recognized and adopted set of guidelines for managing and reducing cybersecurity risk. The NIST CSF is designed to be flexible, providing organizations with a framework for assessing their current cybersecurity posture, identifying gaps in that posture, and developing a road map for improving cybersecurity.

Board members should know that the NIST CSF is organized into three primary components: the Framework Core, the Framework Implementation Tiers, and the Framework Profiles. The Framework Core consists of five functions—Identify, Protect, Detect, Respond, and Recover—that serve as high-level categories for organizing cybersecurity activities. The Implementation Tiers provide a way to assess the rigor and sophistication of an organization's cybersecurity practices, while the Framework Profiles provide a way to tailor the CSF to the specific needs and risk environment of an organization.

The NIST CSF is widely recognized as an effective way to improve an organization's cybersecurity posture, and many industry and regulatory bodies require compliance with the framework. Board members should understand the importance of ensuring that their organization's cybersecurity practices align with the NIST CSF and implementing the framework to reduce the risk of a cybersecurity incident.

Securities Exchange Commission

The Securities Exchange Commission (SEC) plays a pivotal role in ensuring the stability and integrity of the U.S. financial markets. Among the many responsibilities of the SEC, it provides guidance to public companies about their cybersecurity risks and incident disclosure obligations. The SEC emphasizes that all companies, not just technology firms, are potentially vulnerable to cyber threats, stressing that adequate steps should be taken to address these risks to avoid legal, financial, and reputational consequences.

2011 Cybersecurity Disclosure Guidance

In 2011, the SEC issued guidance to public companies regarding their obligations to disclose cybersecurity risks and incidents. This guidance encouraged companies to assess their cyber threat risks and disclose any material risks or incidents to investors. The guidance also prompted companies to develop and implement policies and procedures for preventing, detecting, and evaluating the adequacy of their existing controls against cyberattacks.

2018 Cybersecurity Disclosure Guidance

In 2018, the SEC issued updated guidance to public companies on disclosing cybersecurity risks and incidents. This guidance highlighted the importance of disclosing material cybersecurity risks and incidents promptly and with sufficient detail to enable investors to evaluate the potential impact on the company's operations, financial condition, and results of operations. The SEC also urged companies to disclose the nature, extent, and potential magnitude of cybersecurity risks and the adequacy of preventative actions taken to reduce cybersecurity risks.

2023 Proposal for New Cybersecurity Requirements

In 2023, the SEC proposed new requirements to address cybersecurity risks, specifically targeting broker-dealers, clearing agencies, major security-based swap participants, national securities associations, national securities exchanges, security-based swap data repositories, security-based swap dealers, and transfer agents, collectively known as *market entities*. The proposal emphasized the need for these entities to have protections in place fit for a digital age and would require all market entities to implement policies and procedures reasonably designed to address their cybersecurity risks. Additionally, it proposed new notification and reporting requirements to improve the SEC's ability to obtain information about significant cybersecurity incidents affecting these entities and new public disclosure requirements to enhance transparency about the cybersecurity risks that can potentially cause adverse impacts to U.S. securities markets.

Cybersecurity Incident: JPMorgan Chase

The JPMorgan Chase data breach in 2014 was a significant cybersecurity incident that had far-reaching implications for both the company and its board of directors. The breach compromised the personal

(continued)

(continued)

information of more than 83 million customers, making it one of the largest data breaches in history.

The impact on JPMorgan Chase's board of directors was substantial, triggering a series of actions and changes within the organization. The breach served as a wake-up call, highlighting vulnerabilities in the company's cybersecurity defenses and the potential risks associated with the financial sector. The board recognized the urgent need to address these issues and took immediate steps to enhance cybersecurity measures and protect customer data.

The incident prompted the board of directors to prioritize cybersecurity as a strategic imperative and allocate significant resources to strengthen the organization's cybersecurity posture. The board recognized that protecting customer information was not only crucial for maintaining trust and confidence but also essential for regulatory compliance and mitigating potential financial and reputational damage.

Following the breach, JPMorgan Chase's board engaged in a comprehensive review of its existing security controls, policies, and procedures. The board sought to identify weaknesses and gaps in the company's cybersecurity infrastructure and initiated efforts to enhance its defenses. This involved investing in advanced threat detection and prevention technologies, bolstering incident response capabilities, and improving employee training and awareness programs.

In addition to internal improvements, the board faced increased regulatory scrutiny and oversight in the aftermath of the breach. Regulatory bodies, such as the SEC and the Federal Reserve, closely examined JPMorgan Chase's cybersecurity practices,

(continued)

leading to more stringent compliance requirements and reporting obligations. The board actively collaborated with regulators to ensure compliance with industry regulations and standards to demonstrate its commitment to cybersecurity governance.

The JPMorgan Chase data breach underscored the importance of robust security controls, threat intelligence, and incident response capabilities within the financial sector. The board of directors recognized the need to continuously monitor and adapt its cybersecurity strategies to stay ahead of evolving threats. The board implemented measures to enhance threat detection, incident response readiness, and recovery processes, aligning its cybersecurity efforts with industry best practices.

The breach had broader implications for the financial industry as a whole. It prompted increased collaboration and information sharing among financial institutions, government agencies, and cybersecurity organizations. The board of directors actively participated in industry forums and discussions to share lessons learned and develop collective approaches to combat cyber threats effectively.

Overall, the JPMorgan Chase data breach was a pivotal event that significantly impacted the board of directors and its approach to cybersecurity governance. The breach drove a renewed commitment to protecting customer data, strengthening security controls, and enhancing cyber resilience within the financial institution. The incident highlighted the importance of proactive cybersecurity measures, collaboration with regulators, and continuous improvement to effectively combat cyber threats in the dynamic and evolving digital landscape.

Discussion of Compliance Requirements and Industry Standards

This section will discuss the various compliance requirements and industry standards companies can follow to improve their cybersecurity posture.

Compliance Requirements

The following are compliance requirements.

Sarbanes-Oxley Act

The U.S. Congress enacted the Sarbanes-Oxley Act (SOX) in 2002 in response to several corporate financial scandals. SOX protects shareholders and the public from accounting errors and fraudulent practices in publicly traded companies. It has significant implications for cybersecurity because it requires companies to establish and maintain adequate internal controls over their financial reporting. Specifically, SOX mandates that companies implement and test controls to ensure the integrity of financial information and the confidentiality and availability of the data that supports that information.

From a cybersecurity perspective, board members need to ensure that their company has adequate controls to protect against threats to the confidentiality, integrity, and availability of financial data. In particular, board members should be aware of the need to establish and test controls over access to financial systems and data and controls over changes to economic systems and data.

SOX also has implications for the reporting of cybersecurity incidents. Under Section 404 of SOX, companies must include an assessment of the effectiveness of their internal controls in their annual reports. This includes controls related to cybersecurity. Additionally, under Section 409 of SOX, companies are required to report any material changes in their financial condition or operations on a timely basis, which could include cybersecurity incidents that have a material impact on the company's financial condition.

Board members should work with their management team to ensure that their company complies with SOX cybersecurity requirements. This includes assessing and testing controls over financial reporting and ensuring that adequate reporting mechanisms are in place to report cybersecurity incidents.

In terms of cybersecurity violations related to SOX, one of the best-known cases is the 2017 Equifax data breach. Equifax was found to have violated SOX due to its inadequate internal controls, lack of risk assessments, and failure to properly disclose the breach in a timely manner. As a result, Equifax paid a $1 billion settlement to the SEC and other agencies.

The involvement of the board of directors in the Equifax case was heavily scrutinized. The company's CEO, CIO, and CSO were called to testify before Congress, and there were questions about the board's oversight and knowledge of the breach. The Equifax board faced criticism for its lack of cybersecurity expertise and for not taking more aggressive action to address the company's cybersecurity risks.

Another example of a SOX-related cybersecurity violation is the Target data breach in 2013. Target was found to have violated SOX due to its failure to properly assess and mitigate risks related to its payment systems. Target ultimately paid a $18.5 million settlement to resolve the case.

In both the Equifax and Target cases, the involvement of the board of directors was a topic of discussion and scrutiny. Boards are expected to have strong oversight over companies' internal controls, risk management, and financial reporting, and failing to address cybersecurity risks can result in significant financial and reputational damage.

New York State Department of Financial Services Cybersecurity Regulation

The New York State Department of Financial Services (NYDFS) Cybersecurity Regulation is a set of rules to ensure that regulated financial institutions implement strong cybersecurity practices to protect customer data. The regulation was introduced in March 2017 and has been updated over time. It applies to all licensed, registered, or chartered financial institutions under New York banking, insurance, and financial services laws.

The NYDFS Cybersecurity Regulation requires regulated entities to establish and maintain a cybersecurity program to protect the entity's information systems' confidentiality, integrity, and availability. The program must include a risk assessment, a written cybersecurity policy, periodic cybersecurity training, and an incident response plan.

In addition to the cybersecurity program, the regulation mandates implementing specific cybersecurity measures, such as encryption, access controls, and multifactor authentication. The regulation also requires third-party service providers to implement similar cybersecurity measures.

The NYDFS Cybersecurity Regulation includes a requirement for annual compliance certification by the board of directors or a senior officer of the regulated entity. The accreditation must attest to the entity's compliance with the regulation, and the certification must be based on a review by qualified personnel of the regulated entity.

Boards of directors should ensure that their regulated entities comply with the NYDFS Cybersecurity Regulation. They should also ensure that their regulated entities have implemented the necessary cybersecurity measures to protect customer data and established a culture of cybersecurity throughout the organization. Boards should review their entities' annual certification of compliance and ask management to report on the effectiveness of the cybersecurity program.

Some of the biggest violations of these regulations include the following:

- *First American Financial Corp.*: In 2019, First American Financial Corp, a title insurance and settlement services company, suffered a data breach that exposed more than 800 million customer records. The records included names, Social Security numbers, birth dates, addresses, and driver's license numbers. The breach was caused by a misconfiguration of First American's website that was exploited by a hacker.

    The NYDFS launched an investigation and found that First American had failed to implement appropriate cybersecurity controls and failed to detect the vulnerability that led to the breach. First American was fined $1.4 million for violating the DFS Cybersecurity Regulations.

    The First American Financial Corp. data breach is a reminder that cyberattacks are a real threat to businesses of all sizes. Businesses must take steps to protect themselves from cyberattacks by implementing strong cybersecurity controls and having a plan in place to respond to cyberattacks.

- *Equifax*: In 2017, Equifax, one of the three major credit reporting agencies in the United States, suffered a massive data breach that exposed the personal information of more than 143 million people. The data breach included names, Social Security numbers, birth dates, addresses, and driver's license numbers. The breach was caused by a vulnerability in Equifax's website that was exploited by hackers.

The NYDFS investigated the breach and found that Equifax had failed to implement appropriate cybersecurity controls and failed to patch a known vulnerability that led to the breach. Equifax was fined $1.5 million for violating the DFS Cybersecurity Regulations.

The Equifax data breach was a major wake-up call for the financial industry. It showed that even large, well-established companies can be vulnerable to cyberattacks. The breach also highlighted the importance of strong cybersecurity controls. In the wake of the breach, Equifax has taken steps to improve its cybersecurity program. However, the breach has had a lasting impact on the company's reputation and its customers.

- *Capital One*: In 2019, Capital One, a major credit card company, suffered a data breach that exposed the personal information of more than 100 million customers. The data breach included names, Social Security numbers, birth dates, addresses, and driver's license numbers. The breach was caused by a misconfiguration of Capital One's cloud-based systems that was exploited by a hacker.

  The NYDFS investigated the breach and found that Capital One had failed to implement appropriate cybersecurity controls and failed to detect the vulnerability that led to the breach. Capital One was fined $80 million for violating the DFS Cybersecurity Regulations.

- *Goldman Sachs*: In 2021, the NYDFS fined Goldman Sachs $225 million for failing to adequately protect its customers from cyberattacks. The NYDFS found that Goldman Sachs had a number of deficiencies in its cybersecurity program, including the following:

  - Failing to adequately identify and assess its cybersecurity risks
  - Failing to implement adequate cybersecurity procedures

- Failing to monitor its cybersecurity program for effectiveness
- Failing to have a plan in place to respond to cyberattacks

The NYDFS's fine against Goldman Sachs is the largest ever imposed by the agency for cybersecurity violations. The fine is a significant warning to other financial institutions that they must take cybersecurity seriously.

Financial institutions must have strong cybersecurity programs in place to protect themselves from being hacked.

In each of these cases, the NYDFS found that the companies had failed to implement appropriate cybersecurity controls and failed to detect or address known vulnerabilities. The involvement of the boards of directors in these violations is not clear, but as part of their oversight responsibility, the board should ensure that the company is in compliance with the DFS Cybersecurity Regulations and that appropriate controls and procedures are in place to protect customer information.

Industry Standards

The following are industry standards.

Center for Internet Security Controls

The Center for Internet Security (CIS) Controls are a set of cybersecurity best practices developed by the nonprofit organization The Center for Internet Security. The CIS Controls provide a prioritized framework of action items for organizations to follow to improve their cybersecurity posture. The controls are grouped into three categories—basic, foundational, and organizational—and are regularly updated based on the latest cybersecurity threats and best practices.

As a board member, it is essential to be aware of the CIS Controls because they are widely considered an industry standard for cybersecurity best practices. Familiarity with the CIS Controls can help the board evaluate and improve the organization's cybersecurity program. The CIS Controls can also assess a third-party vendor's cybersecurity program and determine if it is following best practices.

It is recommended that board members work with their IT and cybersecurity teams to understand how the CIS Controls are being implemented within the organization and ensure that the controls are regularly reviewed and updated to reflect the latest best practices. By incorporating the CIS Controls into the organization's cybersecurity program, board members can help to strengthen the organization's overall cybersecurity posture and reduce the risk of cyber incidents.

International Organization for Standardization 27001

International Organization for Standardization (ISO) 27001 is an internationally recognized standard for information security management. It provides a framework for establishing, implementing, maintaining, and continually improving an organization's information security management system (ISMS).

For the board of directors, it is important to understand that adopting the ISO 27001 standard demonstrates an organization's commitment to information security and willingness to follow best practices for managing information security risks. Specifically, the board should be aware that implementing an ISMS based on ISO 27001 can help protect the organization's information assets and minimize the risk of security breaches. The standard provides a structured approach to risk management that can help organizations identify, assess, and manage information security risks.

By adopting ISO 27001, organizations can also demonstrate to their customers and partners that they take information security seriously and have implemented a robust system to manage risks to information security. Furthermore, organizations can undergo a certification process to become ISO 27001 compliant, which can provide additional assurance to stakeholders that the organization is committed to information security. As a result, it is important for board members to understand the importance of ISO 27001 and the benefits it can provide to their organization's cybersecurity posture.

Board members need to understand these compliance requirements and industry standards and work with their IT department or third-party vendors to ensure that their company is in compliance with relevant regulations and standards. By following these requirements and standards, companies can reduce the risk of cyber threats and protect their customers' data. In Chapter 4, we will discuss the role of board members in cybersecurity governance and provide best practices for developing an effective cybersecurity strategy.

Cybersecurity Incident: Activision Blizzard

According to a report by Bloomberg, Activision Blizzard experienced a data breach in 2022 that compromised the personal information of thousands of its employees. The breach was reportedly discovered in February 2022, but the company failed to notify

(continued)

(continued)

its employees until May, violating California's data breach notification law.

The compromised information included employee names, Social Security numbers, addresses, and dates of birth, as well as financial and banking information. The report suggests that the breach may have been carried out by a state-sponsored group based in China. More details are emerging about this attack.

While the exact involvement of the board is not known, the delay in notifying affected employees of the breach could potentially be seen as a failure of oversight and accountability on the part of the board.

Under California law, companies are required to notify affected individuals of a data breach in a timely manner, and the failure to do so can result in legal and financial consequences. The fact that Activision Blizzard waited several months before informing employees of the breach could raise questions about the company's overall approach to cybersecurity and the board's oversight of these efforts.

Individual Director Liability

Individual directors can face significant liability if their company experiences a cybersecurity incident that is not managed correctly. Board members have a legal duty to exercise due care, loyalty, and good faith in carrying out their responsibilities. This includes overseeing the company's cybersecurity posture and ensuring that adequate measures are in place to protect sensitive information.

If a board member fails to fulfill their duty of care by, for example, failing to oversee the company's cybersecurity efforts properly, they can be held liable for any resulting damage. This liability can include financial damages resulting from a data breach or other cyber incident, reputational damage, and loss of business.

Board members can also be held liable for any breaches of data privacy regulations, such as the GDPR or the CCPA. In some cases, they can even face criminal charges if they are found to have intentionally or recklessly ignored cybersecurity risks.

To mitigate these risks, board members should be adequately informed about the company's cybersecurity posture and risk management efforts. They should also ensure that the company has a comprehensive incident response plan and that all employees are properly trained in cybersecurity best practices. Additionally, they should regularly review and update the company's cybersecurity policies and procedures to stay ahead of emerging threats. By taking these steps, board members can help protect the company and themselves from a cybersecurity incident's potential legal and financial consequences.

Here are some of the things that directors can do to protect themselves from individual director liability:

- Attend board meetings regularly, and participate in discussions.
- Ask questions, and make sure they understand the issues being discussed.
- Review and approve all major decisions made by the board.
- Keep up to date on the latest developments in corporate law and governance.
- Seek legal advice if they have any concerns about their legal obligations as a director.

Here are some of the cases where individual directors were held liable for poor cybersecurity management:

- *Yahoo data breach*: Shareholders sued the company's directors for failing to properly oversee and manage the cybersecurity risks facing the company. The directors were accused of failing to implement adequate security measures, failing to disclose the breaches in a timely manner, and failing to properly investigate and address the breaches once they became aware of them.

- *Equifax data breach*: The SEC charged a former Equifax executive with insider trading for selling shares in the company before the public disclosure of the massive data breach that occurred in 2017. The executive was accused of selling shares while in possession of nonpublic information about the breach, which is a violation of securities laws.

- *SolarWinds data breach*: In 2021, a federal jury in California found that the former CEO and former chairman of SolarWinds, a software company, were liable for negligence in the wake of a massive data breach that exposed the company's source code and the source code of its customers. The jury awarded damages of $1.5 billion to the plaintiffs, who included SolarWinds customers and investors.

These cases highlight the potential legal and financial consequences of poor cybersecurity management, including personal liability for executives and directors.

Here are some other things directors can do to protect themselves from individual director liability:

- Ensure that the company has a robust cybersecurity program in place. This program should include a risk assessment, a plan for implementing security controls, and a process for responding to incidents.

- Regularly review the company's cybersecurity program to ensure that it is up to date and effective.
- Stay informed about the latest cybersecurity threats and trends.
- Encourage employees to report any cybersecurity concerns they may have.
- Take steps to mitigate the company's cybersecurity risks, such as implementing strong passwords and multifactor authentication.
- Obtain cybersecurity insurance. This insurance can help protect the company from financial losses in the event of a cybersecurity incident.

By taking these steps, directors can help to protect themselves and the company from the potential legal and financial consequences of a cybersecurity incident.

Cybersecurity Incident: Home Depot

In September 2014, Home Depot experienced a data breach that affected approximately 56 million credit and debit cards. Following the incident, the company faced multiple lawsuits from financial institutions and consumers. In 2017, Home Depot agreed to pay $25 million to settle a lawsuit filed by financial institutions, and in 2019, the company reached a $17.5 million settlement with affected customers.

As for the board of directors, the company faced criticism from some shareholders who argued that the board was not doing enough to address cybersecurity risks. The board eventually created a new

(continued)

(continued)

chief information security officer (CISO) position and appointed a cybersecurity expert to the board's audit committee. Additionally, the board conducted an internal review of its cybersecurity policies and practices and increased investments in cybersecurity measures. In the aftermath of the breach, the company also faced pressure from some shareholders to separate the roles of CEO and chairman, a move that the board ultimately rejected.

Chapter 3 Summary

This chapter delved into the intricate world of cybersecurity regulations and laws, exploring the legal and regulatory environment that organizations must navigate to ensure compliance and mitigate cyber risks. It provided a comprehensive overview of relevant cybersecurity regulations and laws, including federal regulations in the United States, state regulations, European Union regulations, industry standards, and the role of the Securities Exchange Commission in enforcing cybersecurity requirements. Additionally, the chapter discussed compliance requirements, industry standards, and the potential individual director liability related to cybersecurity governance.

The chapter began by highlighting the importance of understanding the legal and regulatory landscape in which organizations operate. It stressed that compliance with cybersecurity regulations is not only a legal obligation but also a critical aspect of effective cybersecurity governance. An overview of relevant cybersecurity regulations and laws was provided to help board members familiarize themselves with the key legal requirements. The chapter explored federal regulations in the United States, which encompass various laws and guidelines aimed at promoting cybersecurity and protecting sensitive information. It also examined state regulations that may impose additional obligations and considerations for organizations operating within specific jurisdictions.

Furthermore, the chapter addressed EU regulations, with a focus on the General Data Protection Regulation. The GDPR has introduced significant changes to data protection practices and has far-reaching implications for organizations that handle personal data of individuals within the EU.

Industry standards play a crucial role in cybersecurity governance, and the chapter emphasized their significance. It highlighted key industry standards, such as the Payment Card Industry Data Security Standard and frameworks provided by the National Institute of Standards and Technology, which offer valuable guidance for organizations to enhance their cybersecurity posture.

The Securities Exchange Commission also plays a role in enforcing cybersecurity requirements for public companies. The chapter explored the SEC's guidance and expectations regarding cybersecurity disclosures, emphasizing the importance of transparency and proactive risk management in the face of cyber threats.

In addition to discussing regulations and industry standards, the chapter delved into compliance requirements and the importance of adhering to them. It emphasized the need for organizations to implement robust compliance programs that align with applicable regulations and standards. By meeting compliance requirements, organizations can demonstrate their commitment to cybersecurity and mitigate legal and reputational risks.

Finally, the chapter touched on individual director liability in the context of cybersecurity governance. It explored the potential legal and regulatory repercussions that board members may face if they fail to fulfill their duties regarding cybersecurity oversight. It highlighted the importance of active board engagement, diligent decision-making, and continuous education to minimize individual director liability risks.

This chapter provided a comprehensive exploration of the legal and regulatory landscape surrounding cybersecurity. By understanding the relevant regulations and laws, compliance requirements, industry standards, and individual director liability risks, board members can effectively fulfill their cybersecurity governance responsibilities. Adhering to legal obligations, embracing industry best practices, and prioritizing compliance contribute to a robust cybersecurity posture and protect organizations from potential legal, financial, and reputational consequences.

Chapter 4

Board Oversight of Cybersecurity

In today's rapidly evolving cyber landscape, boards of directors play a crucial role in ensuring the cybersecurity of their organizations. It is no longer sufficient for cybersecurity to be solely delegated to IT departments or security teams. Boards must actively engage in overseeing their company's cybersecurity strategy and governance framework to effectively mitigate cyber risks and protect their organizations.

This chapter delves into the essential role of the board in overseeing cybersecurity and provides valuable insights and best practices for developing an effective cybersecurity governance framework. By taking proactive measures and embracing their responsibility, boards can ensure that cybersecurity is ingrained into the fabric of their organizations.

We will explore the key components of board oversight, starting with a comprehensive understanding of the risks and threats faced by the organization. By gaining insights into the specific cyber risks and emerging threats, boards can make informed decisions and allocate appropriate resources to strengthen their cybersecurity defenses. We will discuss the development of an effective cybersecurity governance framework. This framework encompasses the policies, processes, and structures that guide cybersecurity efforts across the organization. By establishing a robust governance framework, boards can provide clear direction and ensure that cybersecurity measures are aligned with the organization's strategic objectives.

Effective board engagement and reporting are also critical in cybersecurity governance. Boards must establish mechanisms for regular reporting, enabling them to stay informed about the organization's cybersecurity posture and progress in addressing identified risks. We will delve into best practices for board engagement and reporting, fostering transparent communication and effective oversight.

In the face of potential objections or challenges in addressing cybersecurity at the board level, we will explore strategies for overcoming resistance. By proactively addressing objections, boards can build consensus and encourage a culture of cybersecurity throughout the organization.

This chapter underscores the pivotal role of boards of directors in overseeing cybersecurity. By embracing this responsibility, boards can effectively protect their organizations against cyber threats, respond swiftly to incidents, and foster a culture of cybersecurity awareness. Through the insights and best practices shared in this chapter, boards can position themselves as proactive leaders in the realm of cybersecurity governance.

Cybersecurity Incident: Marriott International

In 2018, Marriott experienced a massive data breach that impacted the personal information of nearly 500 million customers. The breach resulted from a cyberattack on the company's Starwood guest reservation database, which had been compromised in 2014 but was not discovered until 2018. Marriott's board of directors was immediately faced with questions and concerns about the company's cybersecurity practices and response to the incident. The board faced criticism for not taking appropriate measures to protect customer data and not detecting the breach sooner. In the aftermath of the breach, the company's CEO and chief information security officer resigned, and the company faced numerous lawsuits and regulatory investigations. The incident highlighted the need for solid cybersecurity governance and oversight at the board level to protect against data breaches and other cyber threats.

The Board's Role in Overseeing Cybersecurity Strategy

As cyber threats continue to increase in frequency and sophistication, it is vital that boards of directors are actively engaged in overseeing their companies' cybersecurity strategy. This means understanding the organization's risks and threats and ensuring that effective measures are in place to mitigate those risks.

The board's role in cybersecurity strategy includes the following:

- *Setting the tone for the organization's cybersecurity culture*: Boards should establish and promote a culture of cybersecurity within the organization by demonstrating their commitment to cybersecurity and ensuring that it is a priority for the entire organization.
- *Understanding the organization's cybersecurity risks*: Boards should ensure they understand the specific cybersecurity risks the organization faces, including the types of data and systems most vulnerable to cyber threats.
- *Reviewing and approving the cybersecurity strategy*: Boards should review and approve the company's cybersecurity strategy to ensure that it aligns with the organization's overall business objectives and provides adequate protection against cyber threats.
- *Overseeing the implementation of the cybersecurity strategy*: Boards should ensure that management implements the cybersecurity strategy and regularly monitors and updates it as needed.
- *Providing oversight of cybersecurity incidents*: Boards should be prepared to provide oversight and guidance during a cybersecurity incident, including reviewing the response plan and ensuring that appropriate measures are taken to mitigate the incident.
- *Ensuring that appropriate resources are allocated for cybersecurity*: Boards should ensure that adequate resources, including funding and personnel, are allocated to the cybersecurity function to support the effective implementation of the cybersecurity strategy.

Legal Responsibilities

Board members have a legal responsibility to oversee the cybersecurity of their organization. This responsibility is typically outlined in various laws, regulations, and standards that apply to their specific industry or sector.

For example, in the United States, the Sarbanes-Oxley Act of 2002 requires public companies to establish and maintain internal controls over financial reporting, which includes cybersecurity measures to protect financial data. Additionally, many states have data breach notification laws that require companies to notify individuals and government agencies in the event of a breach.

Board members may also face legal liability in the event of a cybersecurity breach if they are found to have failed to fulfill their duty of care, duty of loyalty, or duty of obedience. This can include failing to properly oversee the organization's cybersecurity posture or responding appropriately to a known cybersecurity risk.

Therefore, board members must be knowledgeable about cybersecurity issues, establish policies and procedures for cybersecurity risk management, and ensure that the organization complies with all relevant laws and regulations.

By taking an active role in overseeing their company's cybersecurity strategy, boards can help ensure that their organization is better protected against cyber threats and that appropriate measures are in place to mitigate the risks. In the next section, we will discuss developing an effective cybersecurity governance framework.

Developing an Effective Cybersecurity Governance Framework

To ensure effective oversight of cybersecurity, boards should establish a cybersecurity governance framework. This framework should provide clear guidance on the roles and responsibilities of the board and management regarding cybersecurity, as well as the policies, procedures, and controls necessary to protect the organization against cyber threats.

Here are some critical components of an effective cybersecurity governance framework:

- *Governance structure*: Define the roles and responsibilities of the board, management, and other stakeholders regarding cybersecurity, including how they will work together to implement the cybersecurity strategy.
- *Risk management*: Establish a risk management framework that identifies, assesses, and manages cybersecurity risks, including developing policies, procedures, and controls to mitigate those risks.
- *Incident management*: Develop a comprehensive incident response plan that outlines how the organization will respond to cybersecurity incidents, including the roles and responsibilities of key stakeholders, escalation procedures, and communication plans.
- *Training and awareness*: Ensure that all employees, including the board and management, receive regular training on cybersecurity best practices and are aware of their roles and responsibilities in protecting the organization against cyber threats.
- *Monitoring and reporting*: Establish a monitoring and reporting framework to ensure that the board is regularly informed about the organization's cybersecurity posture and that appropriate measures are taken to address any identified gaps or weaknesses.

By developing a practical cybersecurity governance framework, boards can help ensure that the organization is well-protected against cyber threats and that appropriate measures are in place to respond effectively if a breach does occur. The next section will discuss best practices for board engagement and reporting.

Best Practices for Board Engagement and Reporting

Effective engagement and reporting are critical to the board's effective cybersecurity oversight. The following are some best practices for board engagement and reporting.

Regular Reporting

Boards should receive regular reports on the organization's cybersecurity posture and incidents. Reports should be provided regularly and designed to provide the board with the information it needs to oversee cybersecurity effectively.

Here are some specific reports and information that should be highlighted in regular cybersecurity reports to the board:

- *Threat landscape updates*: Regular updates on the current threat landscape can help the board understand the evolving cybersecurity risks and adjust the organization's security strategy accordingly.
- *Incident response metrics*: Reporting on incident response metrics such as response time, resolution time, and incident severity can help the board understand how effectively the organization is detecting and responding to security incidents.
- *Compliance*: Reports on compliance with relevant regulations and industry standards can help the board understand how well the organization meets its legal and regulatory obligations.
- *Risk assessments*: Reports on regular risk assessments can help the board understand the organization's cybersecurity risks and the effectiveness of the risk management strategy.

- *Third-party risk management*: Reports on third-party risk management can help the board understand the organization's exposure to cybersecurity risks through its relationships with vendors and other third parties.
- *Budget and resource allocation*: Reports on cybersecurity budget and resource allocation can help the board understand how well the organization prioritizes cybersecurity and whether additional investments are needed.
- *Security awareness and training*: Reports on employee security awareness and training can help the board understand how well employees are being educated on cybersecurity risks and whether additional training is needed.

Regular reporting is essential for ensuring that the board has visibility into the organization's cybersecurity posture and can make informed decisions about cybersecurity investments and risk management strategies. These reports should be provided regularly, such as quarterly or annually, and should be tailored to the needs of the board.

Use of Metrics

Reports should include key metrics relevant to the organization's cybersecurity posture. These can include information about the number and type of incidents, control effectiveness, and employee awareness and training level.

Here are some specific metrics that boards should be aware of and monitor:

- *Incident response time*: This metric measures the amount of time it takes for the organization to respond to and resolve a security incident. A longer response time could indicate a weakness in the company's security controls or a lack of resources for incident response.

- *Employee awareness*: Boards should ensure that their employees know cybersecurity risks and are trained to recognize and report potential security incidents. This can be measured by conducting regular security awareness training and phishing simulations.
- *Patch management*: Regularly patching software vulnerabilities is essential for maintaining a solid security posture. Boards should monitor how quickly patches are deployed after being released by software vendors.
- *Threat intelligence*: Monitoring and analyzing external threat intelligence can help boards identify emerging threats and adjust their security strategy accordingly.
- *Compliance*: Compliance with relevant regulations and industry standards is an important aspect of cybersecurity governance. Boards should monitor compliance with the General Data Protection Regulation (GDPR), the Health Insurance Portability and Accountability Act (HIPAA), and Payment Card Industry Data Security Standard (PCI-DSS) regulations and industry standards such as the National Institute of Standards and Technology (NIST) and the International Organization for Standardization (ISO).
- *Cybersecurity budget*: The board should monitor the cybersecurity budget to ensure that it sufficiently addresses the organization's cybersecurity risks. It is important to balance the cost of cybersecurity with the potential threats to the organization.
- *Risk assessments*: Regularly conducting risk assessments can help boards identify potential security weaknesses and prioritize resources for risk mitigation.

These metrics can provide valuable insights into the company's cybersecurity program and help boards make informed decisions about cybersecurity investments and risk management strategies. It is essential to regularly monitor and report on these metrics to ensure that the board can see the company's cybersecurity posture.

Executive Briefings

Boards should receive regular executive briefings from management on the organization's cybersecurity posture and key risks. These briefings should be designed to provide the board with a clear understanding of the risks facing the organization and the steps being taken to mitigate those risks.

Here is a sample meeting agenda for an executive briefing:

- *Introduction and overview*: The session will begin with a brief introduction and overview of the current cybersecurity landscape and the risks facing the organization.
- *Threat landscape*: The next item on the agenda will be a presentation on the current threat landscape, including recent trends and emerging threats.
- *Incident response*: The organization's incident response capabilities will be reviewed, focusing on recent incidents and lessons learned.
- *Compliance*: The briefing will include a review of the organization's compliance posture, including any recent regulatory changes and their impact on the organization.
- *Risk assessment*: A review of the latest risk assessment will be presented, including any identified vulnerabilities or areas of concern.
- *Third-party risk management*: The organization's third-party risk management program will be reviewed, including the current state of vendor risk assessments.
- *Security awareness and training*: The briefing will include a review of the latest security awareness and training initiatives, focusing on recent successes and areas for improvement.

- *Budget and resource allocation*: The session will conclude with a review of the cybersecurity budget and resource allocation, including any recent investments or areas of focus.

The purpose of the executive briefing is to provide the board with a comprehensive overview of the organization's cybersecurity posture and the information needed to make informed decisions about cybersecurity investments and risk management strategies.

Cybersecurity Drills

Boards should participate in cybersecurity drills and exercises to test the organization's incident response plan and identify any areas for improvement.

Here are some examples of the types of cybersecurity drills a board could participate in:

- *Tabletop exercises*: This exercise involves a simulated scenario where board members work together to make decisions and respond to a hypothetical cyberattack. The scenario should be based on a realistic threat, and board members should be encouraged to identify and address gaps in their cybersecurity posture.
- *Incident response drills*: Incident response drills are designed to test the organization's response to a real-time cyberattack. Board members should participate in this exercise to better understand the organization's response capabilities and identify areas for improvement.
- *Red team exercises*: Red team exercises involve hiring an external team to attempt to breach the organization's security defenses. Board members should participate in this type of exercise to gain a better understanding of the organization's vulnerabilities and identify areas for improvement.

- *Compliance audits*: Compliance audits are designed to test the organization's compliance with relevant laws and regulations. Board members should participate in this exercise to ensure that the organization meets its legal and regulatory obligations.

The purpose of these drills is to provide the board with a better understanding of the organization's cybersecurity posture and identify areas for improvement. By participating in these drills, the board can ensure that the organization is better prepared to respond to cyber threats and that the necessary resources are allocated to mitigate cyber risks.

Independent Assessments

Boards should commission independent assessments of the organization's cybersecurity posture to provide an objective view of the organization's risks and threats. When doing so, a board should keep several key considerations in mind. Here are a few:

- *Scope of the assessment*: The board should clearly define the size of the assessment, including the systems, assets, and data that will be included. The board should also consider the type of assessment that best suits the organization's needs, such as a vulnerability assessment, penetration testing, or risk assessment.
- *Qualifications of the assessor*: The board should ensure that the assessor has the appropriate qualifications and experience to conduct the assessment. This includes thoroughly understanding the latest cybersecurity threats, tools, and techniques.
- *Timing of the assessment*: The board should consider the timing of the assessment, including how frequently reviews should be conducted. The frequency of assessments will depend on the organization's risk profile, and

the board should ensure that assessments are conducted regularly.

- *Reporting and communication*: The board should consider how the assessment results will be reported and communicated. The report should clearly outline the findings, including any vulnerabilities or weaknesses identified, and provide recommendations for addressing these issues. The board should also ensure that the information is communicated to the relevant stakeholders and that there is a plan to address any identified issues.
- *Budget*: The board should consider the budget for the assessment and ensure that it is sufficient to cover the cost of the assessment and any necessary remediation activities. The board should also consider the potential return on investment of the assessment, including the potential cost savings that could result from identifying and addressing vulnerabilities before they can be exploited.

By considering these key factors, the board can ensure that independent assessments are conducted effectively and that the organization's cybersecurity posture is continuously improving.

By adopting these best practices, boards can ensure that they are well informed about the organization's cybersecurity posture and that appropriate measures are in place to protect the organization against cyber threats. In the next section, we will discuss overcoming common objections from the management team and other board members.

Overcoming Objections to Effective Cybersecurity Oversight

Effective cybersecurity oversight by boards may require support from the management team or collaboration with other board members. Here are some common objections that boards may encounter and strategies for overcoming them:

- *"Cybersecurity is not a priority for our organization."* Boards should emphasize cybersecurity's critical role in protecting the organization's assets and reputation and that effective oversight of cybersecurity is an essential part of their fiduciary duties.
- *"We don't think we are a likely target for a cyberattack."* Boards should recognize that all organizations, regardless of size or industry, are at risk of a cyberattack and that the cost of a data breach can be high. By implementing effective cybersecurity measures, the organization can reduce the likelihood of a successful attack and minimize the potential impact of a breach.
- *"We don't have the budget or resources to invest in cybersecurity."* Boards should work with management to identify the budgetary resources necessary to implement an effective cybersecurity program and consider the potential financial impact of a cyberattack. In some cases, the cost of a cyberattack can far exceed the cost of investing in cybersecurity measures.
- *"We don't have the expertise to oversee cybersecurity effectively."* Boards should recognize that cybersecurity is a complex and evolving field and that it can take time for organizations to keep up with the latest threats and best practices. By attending training sessions or bringing in outside experts to provide guidance and support, boards can enhance their knowledge of cybersecurity and better fulfill their oversight responsibilities.
- *"We have other priorities that are more important."* Boards should stress that cybersecurity is a critical aspect of the organization's overall risk management strategy and that failing to prioritize cybersecurity could have significant consequences for the organization.

- *"We already have IT staff, so we don't need a cybersecurity expert."* Boards should recognize cybersecurity as a specialized field and that IT staff may need more expertise to address all cybersecurity risks. It may be necessary to bring in additional expertise or to train existing staff in cybersecurity best practices.
- *"We already comply with relevant regulations, so we don't need to do more."* Boards should recognize that compliance with regulations is a minimum standard and that additional measures may be necessary to effectively protect the organization from cyber threats. In addition, regulations may not cover all potential risks, so it is essential to take a comprehensive approach to cybersecurity.
- *"We don't want to inconvenience employees with overly strict security measures."* Boards should recognize that security measures are necessary to protect the organization's assets and reputation and that appropriate security measures can be implemented without inconveniencing employees. It may be helpful to work with management and employees to identify security measures that are effective and practical.

By addressing these objections and concerns, boards can help ensure that the organization is well-protected against cyber threats and that appropriate measures are in place to respond effectively if a breach does occur. The next chapter discusses how boards can work with management to develop an effective cybersecurity strategy.

Promoting a Cybersecurity Culture

As a board member, it is important to recognize that cybersecurity is not just an IT issue but a business issue. *Cybersecurity culture* is a shared set of attitudes, beliefs, behaviors, and values that help organizations protect their assets, minimize risk, and build trust with customers and stakeholders. Promoting a cybersecurity culture requires a top-down approach that involves everyone in the organization, not just the IT department.

Here are some steps board members can take to help develop and promote a culture of cybersecurity:

1. *Create a cybersecurity policy.* Start by developing a cybersecurity policy that outlines the company's expectations for employee behavior and the steps that should be taken in the event of a cybersecurity incident. The policy should be clear, concise, and easily accessible to all employees.

2. *Provide training.* Provide regular cybersecurity training to employees, including how to identify phishing emails, use strong passwords, and recognize potential security risks. This training should be mandatory for all employees, regardless of their role within the organization.

3. *Foster open communication.* Encourage a culture of open communication where employees feel comfortable reporting potential security risks and incidents. This includes providing anonymous reporting channels to protect employees who may be hesitant to come forward.

4. *Hold employees accountable.* Establish clear consequences for employees who violate the company's cybersecurity policy. These can include disciplinary action, termination, and even legal action if necessary.

5. *Lead by example.* Board members and senior executives should lead by example by following cybersecurity policies and best practices and actively promoting a culture of cybersecurity within the organization.

6. *Conduct regular cybersecurity assessments.* Conduct regular cybersecurity assessments to identify potential weaknesses and areas for improvement. These can include vulnerability assessments, penetration testing, and other cybersecurity audits.

By taking these steps, board members can help establish and promote a culture of cybersecurity within their organization. This culture will help protect the company from cyber threats and minimize the risk of data breaches and other cybersecurity incidents.

Chapter 4 Summary

This chapter delved into the crucial topic of board oversight of cybersecurity. As cyber threats continue to evolve and pose significant risks to organizations, boards of directors must play an active role in overseeing their company's cybersecurity strategy. The chapter emphasized the importance of understanding the risks and threats facing the organization and outlined best practices for developing an effective cybersecurity governance framework.

The chapter began by highlighting the changing landscape of cybersecurity and the need for board members to be actively engaged in cybersecurity oversight. It emphasized that cybersecurity is no longer solely the responsibility of IT departments or security teams, but a strategic concern that requires board-level attention and involvement. To effectively oversee cybersecurity, board members must have a comprehensive understanding of the risks and threats faced by the organization. This involves staying informed about the evolving threat landscape, including emerging cyber risks and trends. By gaining insights into the specific cyber risks that their organization faces, board members can make informed decisions and allocate appropriate resources to mitigate those risks.

Developing an effective cybersecurity governance framework was another key focus of the chapter. The framework encompasses the policies, processes, and structures that guide cybersecurity efforts across the organization.

The chapter emphasized the need for boards to establish clear cybersecurity objectives, define roles and responsibilities, and set expectations for management and employees regarding cybersecurity.

Effective board engagement and reporting are critical for cybersecurity governance. The chapter explored best practices for board engagement, emphasizing the importance of establishing regular reporting mechanisms and maintaining open lines of communication with management. It also highlighted the significance of creating a culture of cybersecurity throughout the organization, with board members leading by example and promoting cybersecurity awareness among employees.

In addressing potential objections or challenges related to cybersecurity oversight, the chapter offered strategies for overcoming resistance. It recognized that some board members may have limited technical expertise in cybersecurity and provided guidance on how to bridge this knowledge gap. By addressing objections and fostering a shared understanding of the importance of cybersecurity, boards can drive meaningful change and ensure effective cybersecurity governance.

Overall, this chapter underscored the critical role of boards of directors in overseeing cybersecurity. By embracing this responsibility and implementing the best practices outlined in the chapter, board members can enhance their organization's cybersecurity posture, protect against cyber threats, and position their company for long-term success in the digital age.

Chapter 5
Board Oversight of Cybersecurity: Ensuring Effective Governance

As organizations increasingly rely on digital technologies and face evolving cyber threats, the role of boards of directors in overseeing cybersecurity becomes paramount. In this chapter, we delve into the critical area of board oversight of cybersecurity and explore strategies to ensure effective governance.

Recognizing the significant impact that cyber risks can have on business operations, financial stability, and reputation, this chapter emphasizes the importance of robust risk management and assessment practices. Boards need to understand the potential consequences of cyber risks and the value of proactive risk management in safeguarding their organization.

To effectively oversee cybersecurity, boards must have a comprehensive understanding of the organization's cyber risk landscape. We will explore strategies for identifying, assessing, and prioritizing cyber risks, enabling boards to make informed decisions and allocating appropriate resources to address these risks. From conducting cybersecurity risk assessments to implementing threat intelligence programs and developing risk management frameworks, this chapter provides actionable insights to help boards navigate the complexities of cyber risk. The chapter underscores the need for regular cybersecurity risk assessments as a vital component of effective governance. We will discuss the benefits of conducting periodic assessments to identify vulnerabilities, evaluate controls, and assess the effectiveness of cybersecurity measures. By adopting a proactive approach to risk assessment, boards can stay ahead of emerging threats and ensure the continual improvement of their organization's cybersecurity posture.

The chapter highlights the significance of fostering a culture of cybersecurity throughout the organization. Boards play a critical role in promoting cybersecurity awareness among employees, encouraging best practices, and integrating cybersecurity into the organization's overall risk management framework. By championing a strong cybersecurity culture, boards can enhance the organization's resilience and minimize the likelihood and impact of cyber incidents.

This chapter underscores the pivotal role of boards of directors in ensuring effective governance of cybersecurity. By understanding the impact of cyber risks, implementing robust risk management practices, conducting regular risk assessments, and fostering a cybersecurity-conscious culture, boards can position their organizations to navigate the complex cybersecurity landscape with confidence and resilience.

Cybersecurity Incident: Capital One

In 2019, Capital One was hit by a massive data breach that exposed the personal information of more than 100 million customers. The breach was caused by a misconfigured firewall in the company's cloud environment that allowed the hacker to access sensitive data. The breach led to several regulatory investigations and lawsuits against the company. The company's board of directors was also impacted, with the CEO and CISO testifying before Congress about the breach and the company's response. The incident highlighted the importance of proper cybersecurity controls and oversight from the board level and resulted in changes to the company's security and risk management processes.

The Role of the Board in Overseeing Cybersecurity

As the digital landscape continues to expand and evolve, so do the potential threats to a company's cybersecurity. It is essential that boards have a fundamental understanding of cyber risk and its potential impact on the company's operations.

First, cyber risk should be viewed as a business risk, just like any other operational risk. Boards must recognize that a cyberattack can disrupt operations, damage the company's reputation, and lead to significant financial losses.

The impact of a cyberattack is not limited to the direct financial cost of recovery and remediation. There can also be long-lasting damage to a company's brand and reputation, leading to loss of customer trust and market share. Additionally, cyberattacks can result in legal and regulatory penalties, fines, and other legal liabilities.

To understand the potential impact of cyber risk on the company's operations, the board should ask questions such as these: What are the company's most critical systems and data assets? What is the impact of a cyberattack on these assets, and what are the potential financial and reputational losses that could result? What are the potential regulatory and legal consequences of a cyberattack?

Cybersecurity Incident: UCLA

In 2014, the University of California, Los Angeles (UCLA) suffered a significant cybersecurity incident that resulted in the theft of personal information belonging to 4.5 million individuals. The breach occurred when hackers gained access to a database containing names, Social Security numbers, birth dates, and other personal information for current and former students, faculty, and staff.

According to reports, the attack was initiated through a vulnerability in an application used by the university's administrative office. The breach went undetected for several months until a database administrator discovered unusual activity and reported it to the university's information security team.

In the aftermath of the breach, UCLA faced significant criticism for its handling of the incident. The university was accused of failing to adequately protect sensitive information and delaying

(continued)

(continued)

its notification to affected individuals. The incident also led to a class-action lawsuit against the university.

While it is uncertain what specific role the UCLA board of directors played in this incident, it is likely that board members were involved in overseeing the university's cybersecurity practices and policies. As with any cybersecurity incident, the board would have a responsibility to assess the situation, ensure that appropriate steps were taken to address the breach and prevent future incidents, and communicate with stakeholders about the impact of the breach. If the board was not sufficiently involved in overseeing cybersecurity at the university, the incident may highlight the need for increased oversight and attention to cybersecurity risk management at the board level.

It's important to note that cyber risk is not a static threat. It constantly evolves, and new threats and attack methods are always emerging. Boards should stay informed about the latest trends and developments in the cyber threat landscape to understand how their organization may be affected.

Ultimately, the board should work with management to assess the company's overall cyber risk exposure and establish an appropriate risk tolerance level. This will help guide the company's cybersecurity strategy development and ensure that the right resources are allocated to effectively manage cyber risk.

Developing an Effective Cybersecurity Governance Framework

Board members must comprehensively understand the cyber risks the organization faces. While cyber threats are constantly evolving, several strategies can help boards identify, assess, and prioritize these risks.

Conduct a Cybersecurity Risk Assessment

A cybersecurity risk assessment systematically evaluates the organization's potential risks and vulnerabilities. This assessment should be conducted regularly to ensure that the organization is aware of the latest threats and vulnerabilities. It can also help identify potential weaknesses in the organization's current security posture and provide recommendations for improvement.

Implement a Threat Intelligence Program

A threat intelligence program involves collecting and analyzing information about potential cyber threats. This information can help the organization avoid emerging threats and take proactive measures to mitigate them. A threat intelligence program should be tailored to the organization's needs and regularly reviewed and updated.

Develop a Risk Management Framework

A risk management framework provides a structured approach to managing and mitigating cyber risks. It should include policies, procedures, and guidelines for identifying, assessing, prioritizing, and responding to cyber risks. The framework should be regularly reviewed and updated to remain relevant and effective.

Prioritize High-Impact Risks

Not all cyber risks are created equal. It is crucial to prioritize risks based on their potential impact on the organization. This can help the organization allocate resources more effectively and ensure that it is focusing on the most critical risks first.

Regularly Review and Update Risk Management Strategies

Cyber threats constantly evolve, and boards must regularly review and update their risk management strategies to ensure that they remain effective. This should include regular risk assessments, ongoing threat intelligence gathering, and regular updates to the risk management framework.

Implementing these strategies ensures that the organization is well-equipped to identify, assess, and prioritize cyber risks. This can help the organization allocate resources more effectively and proactively mitigate potential threats.

Cybersecurity Incident: Pearson PLC

In 2018, educational publishing company Pearson PLC suffered a major cybersecurity incident that impacted nearly 1 million student records. The breach involved unauthorized access to a database that contained information such as names, dates of birth, and email addresses. While no financial information or Social Security numbers were compromised, the incident was still a major concern for students and their families, as well as for Pearson PLC.

(continued)

(continued)

The breach was initially detected in March 2018, but it was not until July 2019 that Pearson PLC disclosed the full extent of the incident. The delay in notification was criticized by many, including regulators and affected individuals, as it prevented students and parents from taking timely action to protect themselves from potential identity theft and other consequences of the breach.

The incident also raised questions about the security practices of Pearson PLC and the effectiveness of its cybersecurity program. While the company maintained that it had implemented a comprehensive security program, including regular risk assessments and other measures, it was clear that the program had not been sufficient to prevent the breach.

The involvement of the board of directors in the incident is not clear from public records. However, as with any major cybersecurity incident, it is likely that the board was involved in overseeing the company's response and determining the steps that needed to be taken to prevent similar incidents in the future. The incident serves as a reminder of the critical importance of board oversight of cybersecurity risk management and the need for companies to have effective plans in place to prevent, detect, and respond to cyber threats.

Strategies for Identifying, Assessing, and Prioritizing Cyber Risks

Effective cybersecurity risk management requires a proactive approach to identifying and assessing potential threats and vulnerabilities to an organization. By identifying potential risks and evaluating each risk's likelihood and impact, board members can take steps to mitigate and reduce the likelihood and potential impact of cyberattacks.

To help boards effectively identify, assess, and prioritize cyber risks, several frameworks and best practices can be used, including the following:

- *NIST Cybersecurity Framework*: The National Institute of Standards and Technology (NIST) Cybersecurity Framework is widely adopted for managing cybersecurity risk. The framework provides guidance on how organizations can identify, assess, and manage cybersecurity risk. It includes a set of core functions, including identifying, protecting, detecting, responding, and recovering, and it provides a common language for organizations to communicate cybersecurity risk management.
- *ISO/IEC 27001*: ISO/IEC 27001 is an international standard for information security management systems. The standard provides a framework for managing and protecting sensitive information using risk management processes. The standard is designed to help organizations establish and maintain an effective information security management system.
- *FAIR*: The Factor Analysis of Information Risk (FAIR) model is a quantitative risk management framework that helps organizations understand and quantify cyber risk. The framework provides a common language for risk management and helps organizations make data-driven decisions about risk management.
- *Cybersecurity risk assessments*: Cybersecurity risk assessments involve identifying potential risks and vulnerabilities to an organization's IT systems and evaluating the potential impact of each risk. The assessment should include an analysis of the organization's technology infrastructure, including hardware, software, and

network architecture, and an evaluation of the organization's policies and procedures related to cybersecurity risk management.

It is important for boards to work with management to implement a risk management framework tailored to the organization's specific risk profile and business objectives. By identifying, assessing, and prioritizing cyber risks, board members can better understand their organization's overall risk posture and take steps to mitigate risk and protect the organization from cyberattacks.

Conducting Cybersecurity Risk Assessments

As a board member, a key responsibility is ensuring that the organization has an effective cybersecurity risk management program. One of the key components of such a program is conducting regular cybersecurity risk assessments.

A *cybersecurity risk assessment* is a comprehensive review of an organization's cybersecurity posture, policies, and procedures, intended to identify and prioritize risks to the organization's critical assets and operations.

The board should play a critical role in overseeing the cybersecurity risk assessment process, ensuring that it is conducted regularly and effectively. Board members should be aware of the different types of cybersecurity risk assessments, such as vulnerability assessments, penetration testing, and threat modeling, and the benefits and limitations of each.

To conduct a successful cybersecurity risk assessment, it's important to ensure that the process is thorough and systematic. This includes identifying the critical assets and systems that need to be protected, assessing the likelihood and potential impact of various cyber threats, and identifying the controls and safeguards in place to mitigate risks.

Board members should also be aware of the potential limitations of risk assessments, such as the rapidly changing threat landscape and the possibility of human error or insider threats. It's important to ensure that the risk assessment process is ongoing and adaptable to new threats and challenges.

Here are some of the key steps involved in conducting a cybersecurity risk assessment:

1. *Identify assets and systems.* The first step is to identify the organization's critical assets and systems. These are the assets that are most important to the organization's operations and that would be most damaged if they were compromised.

2. *Assess threats.* The next step is to assess the threats that could impact the organization's critical assets and systems. This includes identifying the different types of threats, such as malware, phishing, and data breaches, and assessing the likelihood and potential impact of each threat.

3. *Identify controls.* The next step is to identify the controls that are in place to mitigate the risks to the organization's critical assets and systems. These controls can include technical controls, such as firewalls and intrusion detection systems, and administrative controls, such as security policies and procedures.

4. *Assess the effectiveness of controls.* The final step is to assess the effectiveness of the controls that are in place to mitigate the risks to the organization's critical assets and systems. This includes identifying any gaps in the controls and making recommendations for improvement.

Conducting cybersecurity risk assessments is a critical component of an effective cybersecurity risk management program. Board members should actively oversee the process and ensure that the organization takes appropriate measures to mitigate cybersecurity risks.

Here are some additional tips for board members on conducting cybersecurity risk assessments:

- *Get input from all levels of the organization.* The cybersecurity risk assessment process should involve input from all levels of the organization, including the board, senior management, IT staff, and employees. This will help to ensure that the assessment is comprehensive and takes into account the perspectives of all stakeholders.
- *Use a variety of tools and techniques.* Various tools and techniques can be used to conduct cybersecurity risk assessments. The best approach will vary depending on the size and complexity of the organization.
- *Keep the assessment process ongoing.* The cybersecurity threat landscape is constantly evolving, so it's important to keep the assessment process ongoing. This will help to ensure that the organization is always aware of the latest threats and takes appropriate measures to mitigate them.

How to Develop and Promote a Culture of Cybersecurity

Developing and promoting a culture of cybersecurity is essential for protecting a company's sensitive data and intellectual property. A company's board plays a critical role in establishing and promoting such a culture. To create a culture of cybersecurity, the board should consider the following steps.

1. The board should establish a cybersecurity policy that outlines the company's commitment to cybersecurity and its expectations for employees. This policy should be communicated clearly and consistently to all employees, and it should be included in employee onboarding and training programs.

2. The board should ensure that the company has the necessary resources to implement and maintain effective cybersecurity practices. This includes investing in cybersecurity technology and tools, as well as hiring qualified cybersecurity professionals who can implement and manage these tools.

3. The board should prioritize cybersecurity in the company's risk management program. This includes regularly assessing and identifying potential cybersecurity risks, as well as developing and implementing strategies to mitigate these risks.

4. The board should promote a culture of cybersecurity awareness and education. This includes regular cybersecurity training for all employees, as well as ongoing communication about cybersecurity risks and best practices. The board can also encourage employees to report potential security incidents or vulnerabilities and provide channels for doing so.

5. The board should lead by example and promote a culture of cybersecurity from the top down. This includes ensuring that board members and executives are aware of cybersecurity risks and best practices, as well as taking responsibility for the company's overall cybersecurity posture.

6. The board should regularly review and assess the effectiveness of the company's cybersecurity culture and policies. This includes tracking key metrics and implementing changes as needed to ensure that the company's cybersecurity posture remains strong.

Developing and promoting a culture of cybersecurity is essential for protecting a company's sensitive data and intellectual property. The board plays a critical role in establishing and promoting such a culture, and it should take a proactive approach to ensure that the company has the necessary resources, policies, and practices in place to prevent cyber threats. By prioritizing cybersecurity, promoting awareness and education, and leading by example, the board can help create a culture of cybersecurity that will protect the company from cyber threats and promote long-term success.

Chapter 5 Summary

As organizations increasingly rely on digital technologies and face evolving cyber threats, the role of boards of directors in overseeing cybersecurity becomes paramount. In this chapter, we delved into the critical area of board oversight of cybersecurity and explored strategies to ensure effective governance.

Recognizing the significant impact that cyber risks can have on business operations, financial stability, and reputation, this chapter emphasized the importance of robust risk management and assessment practices. Boards need to understand the potential consequences of cyber risks and the value of proactive risk management in safeguarding their organization.

To effectively oversee cybersecurity, boards must have a comprehensive understanding of the organization's cyber risk landscape. We explored strategies for identifying, assessing, and prioritizing cyber risks, enabling boards to make informed decisions and allocate appropriate resources to address these risks. From conducting cybersecurity risk assessments to implementing threat intelligence programs and developing risk management frameworks, this chapter provided actionable insights to help boards navigate the complexities of cyber risk.

This chapter also underscored the need for regular cybersecurity risk assessments as a vital component of effective governance. We discussed the benefits of conducting periodic assessments to identify vulnerabilities, evaluate controls, and assess the effectiveness of cybersecurity measures. By adopting a proactive approach to risk assessment, boards can stay ahead of emerging threats and ensure the continual improvement of their organization's cybersecurity posture.

Additionally, the chapter highlighted the significance of fostering a culture of cybersecurity throughout the organization. Boards play a critical role in promoting cybersecurity awareness among employees, encouraging best practices, and integrating cybersecurity into the organization's overall risk management framework. By championing a strong cybersecurity culture, boards can enhance the organization's resilience and minimize the likelihood and impact of cyber incidents.

We stressed the pivotal role of boards of directors in ensuring effective governance of cybersecurity. By understanding the impact of cyber risks, implementing robust risk management practices, conducting regular risk assessments, and fostering a cybersecurity-conscious culture, boards can position their organizations to navigate the complex cybersecurity landscape with confidence and resilience.

Chapter 6

Incident Response and Business Continuity Planning

In today's rapidly evolving digital landscape, organizations face an ever-increasing number of sophisticated cyber threats and attacks. These threats can disrupt operations, compromise sensitive data, and damage a company's reputation. To navigate this challenging landscape, businesses must have robust incident response and business continuity plans in place. This chapter delves into the critical aspects of incident response and business continuity planning, providing comprehensive insights into the implementation of cybersecurity policies and procedures to mitigate risks effectively.

We begin by exploring the importance of implementing cybersecurity policies and procedures throughout an organization. Cybersecurity policies serve as the foundation for establishing a proactive cybersecurity posture. They provide guidelines and rules for employees to follow, ensuring that security measures are consistently applied across the organization. These policies cover areas such as access controls, data protection, incident reporting, employee training, and vendor management. By enforcing these policies, organizations can reduce vulnerabilities and enhance their overall cybersecurity resilience.

The chapter then delves into the core components of incident response and business continuity planning. Organizations must be prepared to handle security incidents promptly and efficiently to minimize the impact on their operations and mitigate potential damage. Incident response planning involves developing comprehensive strategies, workflows, and communication protocols to detect, contain, eradicate, and recover from security incidents effectively. It encompasses various activities, including incident identification and reporting, incident analysis, containment and eradication, evidence gathering, system restoration, and post-incident analysis. By establishing a well-defined incident response plan, organizations can ensure a coordinated and swift response, minimizing the potential harm caused by cyber incidents.

The chapter sheds light on various types of assessments that organizations can conduct to identify vulnerabilities, assess risks, and enhance their cybersecurity posture. These assessments play a crucial role in proactively identifying weaknesses and prioritizing remediation efforts. They include penetration testing, which simulates real-world attacks to identify system vulnerabilities; vulnerability scanning, which scans systems for known vulnerabilities; security risk assessments, which evaluate the organization's overall risk landscape; threat modeling, which helps identify potential threats and their impact; social engineering assessments, which test employee susceptibility to manipulation; compliance assessments, which ensure adherence to regulatory requirements; and red team/blue team exercises, which simulate attack scenarios to test the effectiveness of defenses. By using these assessment methodologies, organizations can gain valuable insights into their security strengths and weaknesses, enabling them to make informed decisions and allocate resources effectively.

This chapter emphasizes the significance of establishing and implementing robust cybersecurity policies and procedures within an organization. It highlights the need for proactive incident response and business continuity planning to effectively handle security incidents and ensure the smooth continuation of operations. Additionally, it explores the different assessment techniques that organizations can use to identify vulnerabilities and enhance their cybersecurity posture. By adopting a comprehensive and proactive approach to incident response and business continuity planning, organizations can bolster their resilience against cyber threats, minimize potential disruptions to their operations, and safeguard their valuable assets and reputation.

Cybersecurity Incident: Garmin

In July 2020, Garmin, the GPS navigation and wearable technology company, was hit by a ransomware attack that impacted many of its online services, including its customer support call centers, production lines, and aviation databases. The incident left the company's systems inoperable, resulting in widespread service disruptions and lost business.

As Garmin is a private company, it is not clear how the Garmin board of directors was explicitly

(continued)

(continued)

impacted by the cybersecurity incident, as the company did not provide detailed information on the matter. However, given the severity of the attack and the significant impact on the company's operations, it is likely that the board was involved in overseeing the company's response and recovery efforts. The incident also highlighted the importance of robust cybersecurity measures and risk management for the board to consider moving forward.

Implementing Cybersecurity Policies and Procedures

As a board member, ensuring that the organization has well-defined cybersecurity policies and procedures is crucial. Effective policies and procedures can help prevent cyberattacks, reduce the impact of successful attacks, and mitigate the damage caused by breaches. In this section, we will discuss the key elements of effective cybersecurity policies and procedures, including the following:

- *Establishing a risk management framework*: A risk management framework helps identify, assess, and prioritize cyber risks to the organization. It provides a systematic approach to understanding the organization's risk exposure and making informed decisions about cybersecurity investments and risk mitigation strategies.
- *Developing a comprehensive cybersecurity policy*: An effective cybersecurity policy is critical to an organization's cybersecurity program. It should define the organization's security objectives, roles, responsibilities, and

controls. The policy should also be reviewed and updated regularly to ensure that it is current and effective.

- *Implementing security controls*: Using security controls is essential to protect the organization's critical assets. Selecting the right security controls based on the organization's risk profile, budget, and operational requirements is important.
- *Conducting cybersecurity awareness training*: Human error contributes significantly to successful cyberattacks. Therefore, it is essential to provide cybersecurity awareness training to employees to promote a culture of cybersecurity.
- *Conducting regular cybersecurity testing*: Regular testing of an organization's cybersecurity controls can help identify vulnerabilities and ensure that controls are operating as intended.

In the following sections, we will provide more detailed guidance on these key elements to help boards implement effective cybersecurity policies and procedures within their organization.

Incident Response and Business Continuity Planning

Board members play a critical role in ensuring that their organization is prepared for and can effectively respond to a cyber incident. Cyber incidents can have a significant impact on an organization's operations, finances, and reputation. By having a comprehensive incident response and business continuity plan in place, the board can help the organization minimize the impact of a cyber incident and recover quickly.

Incident Response Plan

An *incident response plan* is a document that outlines the steps an organization will take in the event of a cyber incident. The plan should include the following:

- *Who should be contacted*: Identify the key individuals who should be contacted in the event of a cyber incident, such as the CEO, CIO, legal counsel, and public relations representative.
- *What actions should be taken*: The plan should outline the specific steps that will be taken in the event of a cyber incident, such as how to contain the incident, investigate the incident, and restore systems and data.
- *How communication with stakeholders should be managed*: The plan should outline how to communicate with stakeholders, such as employees, customers, and investors, in the event of a cyber incident.

Business Continuity Planning

A *business continuity plan* is a document that outlines how the organization will continue to operate in the event of a cyber incident. The plan should do the following:

- *Identify key business processes and systems*: Identify the key business processes and systems that are essential for the organization to continue operating.
- *Prioritize recovery*: Prioritize the recovery of key business processes and systems.
- *Develop alternative solutions*: Develop alternative solutions that can be used if key business processes and systems are unavailable.

Board members should be involved in reviewing and approving the organization's incident response and business continuity plans. This includes ensuring that the plans are comprehensive and up to date and that they include key stakeholders. Board members should also ensure that the plans are regularly reviewed and tested.

By taking these steps, board members can help their organization minimize the impact of a cyber incident and maintain critical operations. Here are some additional tips for board members on incident response and business continuity planning:

- *Get input from all levels of the organization.* The incident response and business continuity planning process should involve input from all levels of the organization, including the board, senior management, IT staff, and employees. This will help to ensure that the plans are comprehensive and that they take into account the perspectives of all stakeholders.
- *Use a variety of tools and techniques.* Various tools and techniques can be used to develop incident response and business continuity plans. The best approach will vary depending on the size and complexity of the organization.
- *Keep the plans up to date.* The cybersecurity threat landscape is constantly evolving, so it's important to keep the incident response and business continuity plans up to date. This will help to ensure that the plans are effective in mitigating the latest threats.

Incident Response Planning

Incident response planning is a critical component of cybersecurity. No matter how much time and effort are invested in cybersecurity measures, it is still possible that an incident may occur. In fact, it's not a question of "if" but "when" a cyberattack will happen. Given this inevitability, it is essential that organizations have an incident response plan in place to respond to and recover from such events.

Board members play a critical role in incident response planning. They should be aware of the key elements of the organization's incident response plan, including the roles and responsibilities of various stakeholders, communication protocols, and escalation procedures. They should also be involved in testing and validating the plan to ensure that it is effective and up to date.

The following are some key considerations for incident response planning that board members should keep in mind:

- *Incident response team*: Organizations should establish an incident response team (IRT) that includes key stakeholders from different areas of the organization. IRT members should clearly understand their roles and responsibilities, and the team should be prepared to respond quickly and effectively to any incident.

- *Communication protocols*: Effective communication is critical during an incident. The incident response plan should include clear communication protocols that outline how the information will be shared, who will be responsible for communicating with various stakeholders, and what information needs to be communicated.

- *Escalation procedures*: The incident response plan should include escalation procedures that outline when and how to escalate an incident to senior management, legal counsel, or law enforcement, as needed.

- *Testing and validation*: Incident response plans should be tested and validated regularly to ensure that they are effective and up to date. This can be done through tabletop exercises or simulated incidents.

- *Continuous improvement*: Incident response planning should be an ongoing process. Board members should ensure that the organization continuously improves its incident response plan to keep up with the evolving threat landscape.

Incident response planning is a critical component of cybersecurity, and board members play a vital role in ensuring that their organization is prepared to respond to and recover from cyber incidents. By understanding the key elements of incident response planning, board members can help their organization better protect itself and minimize the impact of any incidents that occur.

Cybersecurity Incident: Target

Following the cybersecurity breach at Target in 2013, which compromised the personal information of millions of customers, the company's board of directors faced criticism for its handling of the incident. The board was scrutinized for failing to ensure adequate cybersecurity measures and overreacting to the breach.

The breach led to a decline in Target's stock price, and the company faced numerous lawsuits and investigations from regulators. In the aftermath of the breach, the company's CEO and several other senior executives resigned or were replaced.

In 2017, Target agreed to pay $18.5 million to settle a lawsuit brought by 47 states and the District of Columbia over the data breach. The settlement included a requirement for Target to implement a comprehensive information security program and hire an executive to oversee the program.

The Target breach serves as a cautionary tale for boards of directors about the importance of cybersecurity and the need for proactive measures to protect companies and customers. It also highlights the potential legal and financial consequences of adequately addressing cybersecurity risks.

Defining the Types of Assessments

A board member should know about the following types of assessments in the context of cybersecurity risk management.

Penetration Testing

A *penetration test*, also known as a *pen test*, is a simulated cyberattack against a computer system, network, or web application to identify vulnerabilities an attacker could exploit. The test is conducted by a team of ethical hackers, or penetration testers, who use a variety of methods and tools to identify vulnerabilities and attempt to exploit them to gain access to sensitive data or systems.

During a penetration test, the testers attempt to replicate the methods and techniques used by real-world attackers, such as social engineering, phishing, and brute-force attacks. They also use specialized tools to scan for vulnerabilities and attempt to exploit them, with the goal of providing a comprehensive understanding of the organization's security posture.

As a board member, it is important to understand the purpose and scope of a penetration test. The test is designed to identify vulnerabilities in the organization's systems and processes and provide remediation recommendations. The results of a penetration test can help the board understand the risks the organization faces and make informed decisions about cybersecurity investments and priorities.

When presented with the results of a penetration test, it is important for the board to pay attention to the severity and impact of the vulnerabilities identified. It is also important to understand the recommended remediation steps and ensure that appropriate action is taken to address any identified issues. Additionally, the board should ensure that regular penetration testing is conducted to maintain a strong security posture and that the results are regularly reviewed and addressed.

Vulnerability Scanning

Vulnerability scanning is a key component of any comprehensive cybersecurity program. It involves the use of specialized software tools to scan computer networks, systems, and applications to identify potential security weaknesses or vulnerabilities.

The purpose of a vulnerability scan is to identify vulnerabilities that could be exploited by attackers to gain unauthorized access to systems or steal sensitive data. The scanning process involves automated testing of system configurations, open ports, services, and applications to identify vulnerabilities, such as missing patches or unsecured settings. The results of a vulnerability scan can help an organization prioritize its efforts to address security weaknesses and improve its overall security posture.

As a board member, it is important to understand the nature of vulnerability scanning and its importance in maintaining the organization's security. Board members should understand the risks and the potential impact of a cyberattack on the company's reputation, financial performance, and legal liability. They should also understand the role of vulnerability scanning in identifying potential security risks and helping the organization mitigate those risks.

When presented with the results of a vulnerability scan, board members should ensure that they understand the scope and purpose of the scan, as well as the methodology and criteria used for the assessment. They should also pay close attention to any critical or high-risk vulnerabilities identified by the scan and ask questions about how these vulnerabilities will be addressed.

Board members should ensure that the organization has a process in place to track and prioritize vulnerabilities and that the appropriate teams are working to remediate them in a timely manner. They should also ensure that the organization has a plan in place for ongoing vulnerability management, including regular vulnerability scans and follow-up remediation efforts.

Vulnerability scanning is a critical component of any organization's cybersecurity program, and board members should be familiar with the concept and its importance in maintaining the security of the organization.

Cybersecurity Incident: Colonial Pipeline

In May 2021, Colonial Pipeline, a major fuel pipeline operator in the United States, was hit by a ransomware attack that forced the company to shut down its pipeline, leading to fuel shortages in several states. The incident significantly impacted Colonial Pipeline's board of directors, as board members were held responsible for the company's response to the attack. The board was criticized for failing to implement adequate cybersecurity measures and being unprepared to respond to such an incident. The CEO of Colonial Pipeline testified before the U.S. Senate that the board was informed of the incident just hours after it occurred and that the company's cybersecurity plan still needed to be thoroughly tested before the attack. As a result of the incident,

(continued)

(continued)

several members of Colonial Pipeline's board of directors resigned or were replaced. The incident raised concerns about the broader vulnerability of critical infrastructure to cyberattacks.

Security Risk Assessments

A *security risk assessment* is a comprehensive evaluation of an organization's security posture designed to identify potential risks and vulnerabilities to the confidentiality, integrity, and availability of its assets. The assessment is a critical process that enables an organization to identify its most valuable assets, the security controls protecting those assets, and the potential risks and vulnerabilities to those assets.

The assessment process typically includes evaluating the organization's technical, physical, and administrative security controls, as well as its policies, procedures, and governance. This includes an analysis of the current security posture, identification of potential threats and vulnerabilities, and recommendations for improving the overall security posture.

The security risk assessment should be conducted on a regular basis and is an essential component of an organization's overall risk management program. The results of the assessment should be reviewed by the board of directors, which is responsible for ensuring that the organization is appropriately managing risk and that the security program is aligned with the organization's business objectives.

When presented with the results of a security risk assessment, board members should pay particular attention to the key findings and recommendations. These may include specific risks and vulnerabilities that have been identified, as well as the effectiveness of the organization's security controls in mitigating those risks. Board members should also look for any areas where the organization may be out of compliance with relevant regulations or industry standards.

It is essential that board members understand the importance of the security risk assessment and its role in helping the organization identify and manage security risks effectively. By prioritizing the security of its assets and pro-actively identifying potential risks and vulnerabilities, the organization can better protect itself against cyber threats and reduce the potential impact of a security incident.

Threat Modeling

Threat modeling is a process used to identify and evaluate potential threats to an organization's systems, applications, and data. It is a systematic approach to understanding the risks and vulnerabilities of the organization's assets and the ways in which attackers may exploit them. Threat modeling aims to help organizations proactively manage cybersecurity risks and develop appropriate countermeasures.

When presented with the results of a threat modeling exercise, board members should understand the various threats that have been identified and the risks associated with each threat. Threats may include external factors, such as hackers or state-sponsored attackers and internal actors, such as employees or contractors. Board members should be informed about the likelihood and potential impact of each threat and the security measures in place to mitigate those risks.

Threat modeling can be an important tool for board members to understand the cybersecurity risks that their organization faces and the potential impact of those risks. By using this process, organizations can better prioritize their security efforts and allocate resources to areas of greatest need. Board members should work with their cybersecurity team to ensure that regular threat modeling exercises are conducted and the results are communicated clearly and understandably.

Social Engineering Assessments

A *social engineering assessment* is a type of security assessment that tests an organization's susceptibility to social engineering attacks. Social engineering is the art of manipulating people into divulging confidential information, providing access to restricted areas, or performing an action that aids an attacker. This type of assessment is conducted to identify and mitigate the risk of social engineering attacks and to evaluate the effectiveness of an organization's security awareness training program.

During a social engineering assessment, an external or internal security team may attempt to deceive employees into providing sensitive information or access. This can include phishing attacks, phone scams, or physical impersonation. The goal is to test the effectiveness of an organization's security protocols and identify areas of weakness.

When presented with the results of a social engineering assessment, board members should be aware of the types of attacks that were attempted and the level of success the attackers had. It is important to understand which employees were susceptible to the attacks and what sensitive information or access was compromised. Board members should also be aware of any gaps in security awareness training or policies that were identified during the assessment. This information can be used to improve the organization's security posture and prevent future attacks. It is important for board members to understand the urgency and severity of the situation, as a successful social engineering attack can have serious consequences for the organization, including reputational damage and financial losses.

Compliance Assessments

These are assessments of an organization's compliance with relevant cybersecurity regulations and industry standards such as the General Data Protection Regulation (GDPR) and the Payment Card Industry Data Security Standard (PCI DSS). This type of assessment helps identify gaps or vulnerabilities in an organization's compliance program, allowing the organization to take corrective action to improve its compliance posture.

A compliance assessment typically involves a review of policies, procedures, and documentation, as well as interviews with key personnel to assess the compliance program's effectiveness. The assessment may also include testing to verify compliance with specific regulatory or industry requirements.

As a board member, it is important to understand the results of a compliance assessment to ensure that the organization is meeting all legal and regulatory obligations. The assessment may reveal areas where the organization is falling short, such as incomplete documentation, inadequate training, or lack of controls to mitigate risks. The board can then work with management to address these issues and implement corrective actions to improve the organization's compliance posture.

It is also important for the board to be aware of any potential consequences of noncompliance, such as fines or legal action, and to ensure that the organization has adequate resources and processes to maintain compliance over time. This includes regular monitoring and review of the compliance program and ongoing training and awareness for employees and other stakeholders.

A compliance assessment provides valuable insight into an organization's adherence to legal and regulatory requirements and can help the board ensure that the organization is fulfilling its obligations and mitigating risks related to noncompliance.

Red Team/Blue Team Exercise

A *red team/blue team exercise* is a security testing methodology that involves creating two teams: the red team and the blue team. The *red team*, acting as the attackers, attempts to penetrate the organization's security defenses and access sensitive data or systems. The *blue team*, acting as the defenders, works to detect and respond to the red team's attacks.

A red team/blue team exercise aims to simulate a real-world attack and assess an organization's ability to detect and respond to such an attack. The exercise can identify weaknesses in an organization's security controls, policies, and procedures and provide valuable insights into the effectiveness of its security program.

When presented with the results of a red team/blue team exercise, board members should be aware of the following:

- *The scope and objectives of the exercise*: Board members should understand the exercise's goals and the targeted systems or data.
- *The methodologies and techniques used by the red team*: Board members should have a basic understanding of the tools and tactics used by the red team to penetrate the organization's defenses.
- *The effectiveness of the blue team*: Board members should be aware of how the blue team performed in detecting and responding to the red team's attacks. This can help the board assess the strength of the organization's security program.
- *The identified weaknesses and recommendations for improvement*: Board members should be informed about any vulnerabilities or weaknesses that were identified

during the exercise and the recommended remediation steps. This can help the board prioritize investments in security controls and resources.

A red team/blue team exercise can be an effective tool for assessing an organization's security program and identifying potential vulnerabilities. Board members should ensure that the exercise is properly scoped and that the results are presented in a clear and actionable manner.

Board members should understand these types of assessments and their value in identifying and mitigating cybersecurity risks.

Chapter 6 Summary

This chapter delved into the critical aspects of incident response and business continuity planning in the context of cybersecurity. It emphasized the importance of implementing cybersecurity policies and procedures throughout the organization and highlighted the key components of incident response and business continuity planning.

The chapter began by stressing the significance of cybersecurity policies as the foundation for a proactive cybersecurity posture. These policies provide guidelines and rules for employees to follow, covering various areas such as access controls, data protection, incident reporting, employee training, and vendor management. By enforcing these policies, organizations can reduce vulnerabilities and enhance their overall cybersecurity resilience.

Next, the chapter explored the core components of incident response planning. It emphasized the need for organizations to be well-prepared to handle security incidents promptly and efficiently. Incident response planning involves developing comprehensive strategies, workflows, and communication protocols to detect, contain, eradicate, and recover from security incidents effectively. By establishing a well-defined incident response plan, organizations can ensure a coordinated and swift response, minimizing the potential harm caused by cyber incidents.

The chapter highlighted the importance of various types of assessments in enhancing cybersecurity. These assessments enable organizations to identify vulnerabilities, assess risks, and make informed decisions to strengthen their security posture. The assessments discussed included penetration testing, vulnerability scanning, security risk assessments, threat modeling, social engineering assessments, compliance assessments, and red team/blue team exercises. Using these assessment methodologies helps organizations gain valuable insights into their security strengths and weaknesses, enabling them to allocate resources effectively and prioritize remediation efforts.

In conclusion, this chapter emphasized the significance of robust incident response and business continuity planning in the face of evolving cyber threats. It underscored the need for proactive cybersecurity measures, including the implementation of cybersecurity policies, well-defined incident response plans, and various assessments to enhance an organization's cybersecurity posture. By adopting these measures, organizations can effectively handle security incidents, ensure the smooth continuation of operations, and strengthen their resilience against cyber threats.

Chapter 7

Vendor Management and Third-Party Risk

This chapter delves into the critical topic of vendor management and third-party risk in the context of cybersecurity. In today's interconnected business landscape, organizations often rely on third-party vendors and service providers to fulfill various functions. While these partnerships bring many benefits, they also introduce inherent cybersecurity risks. This chapter explores the importance of third-party risk management for board members and outlines best practices for effectively managing and mitigating third-party cyber risks.

The chapter begins by emphasizing the significance of third-party risk management for board members. Board members play a crucial role in overseeing the organization's cybersecurity efforts, and third-party risk management is an essential aspect of this responsibility. By understanding the potential risks associated with third-party relationships, board members can ensure that adequate controls and safeguards are in place to protect the organization's sensitive data and critical systems.

Next, the chapter delves into best practices for managing third-party cyber risks. It highlights the importance of establishing a robust vendor management program that includes comprehensive due diligence processes, contractual obligations, and ongoing monitoring and assessment of third-party vendors. The chapter provides insights into key areas of focus, such as vendor selection, contract negotiation, security assessments, incident response planning, and termination protocols. By following these best practices, organizations can strengthen their resilience to third-party cyber risks and enhance their overall cybersecurity posture.

Furthermore, the chapter explores the legal and regulatory considerations involved in third-party risk management. It emphasizes the need for organizations to align their vendor management practices with relevant laws and regulations to ensure compliance. Additionally, the chapter provides a set of sample questions that board members can ask third-party vendors to assess their cybersecurity capabilities and risk management practices. These questions serve as a valuable tool to evaluate vendors' cybersecurity posture and make informed decisions about their selection and ongoing engagement.

This chapter highlights the criticality of effective vendor management and third-party risk management in the realm of cybersecurity. It underscores the importance of board members' involvement in overseeing third-party relationships and ensuring the implementation of best practices. By actively managing third-party cyber risks, organizations can protect their sensitive information, maintain the trust of their stakeholders, and safeguard their overall cybersecurity resilience.

Cybersecurity Incident: SolarWinds

The SolarWinds cybersecurity incident, discovered in December 2020, affected private and public organizations. The cyberattack involved a supply chain compromise of SolarWinds' Orion software, allowing the attacker to access customer networks. In the aftermath of the incident, SolarWinds' board of directors faced scrutiny for their oversight of the company's cybersecurity posture. The company's CEO, Sudhakar Ramakrishna, stated that it was "clearly not doing enough" to secure its products and pledged to make improvements. SolarWinds faced multiple lawsuits and investigations, including a class-action lawsuit filed by investors who claimed that the company misled them about its cybersecurity practices. SolarWinds has since changed its board, including appointing a new chairperson and three independent directors with cybersecurity and risk management expertise.

The Importance of Third-Party Risk Management for Board Members

As a board member, it is important to recognize that the organization's cybersecurity posture is not limited to its internal controls and infrastructure. Third-party vendors, partners, and service providers can introduce significant risks to the company's cybersecurity, making third-party risk management a crucial component of the overall cybersecurity strategy.

The potential consequences of a third-party cyber breach can be severe, ranging from data breaches and theft of sensitive information to business interruptions and reputational damage. As a board member, it is critical to understand the impact of third-party risks on the company and the steps that can be taken to mitigate those risks.

This section will provide an overview of the importance of third-party risk management for board members, including the following:

- Understanding the risks associated with third-party relationships
- Identifying and assessing third-party risks
- Establishing policies and procedures for third-party risk management
- Integrating third-party risk management into the organization's overall cybersecurity strategy
- Monitoring and reporting on third-party risk management activities

By the end of this chapter, board members should have a solid understanding of the importance of third-party risk management and the key considerations for establishing an effective program.

Best Practices for Managing Third-Party Cyber Risk

As companies increasingly rely on third-party vendors for critical functions, it is important for board members to be aware of the best practices for managing third-party cyber risk. Some key considerations include the following:

- *Conducting due diligence*: Board members should ensure that vendors are thoroughly vetted and evaluated before entering into any contracts. This includes assessing the vendor's cybersecurity posture, security controls, and incident response capabilities.

- *Setting clear security expectations*: Board members should establish clear security expectations with vendors, including requirements for data encryption, access controls, and incident reporting.
- *Monitoring and assessing vendor performance*: Board members should continuously monitor vendor performance to ensure that security standards are being met. This includes regular vulnerability scans and assessments of vendor compliance with security policies.
- *Developing incident response plans*: Board members should work with vendors to develop incident response plans and ensure that they are tested and reviewed regularly. This can help minimize the impact of any potential security incidents.
- *Contracting for cyber insurance*: Board members should ensure that contracts with vendors include requirements for cyber insurance coverage. This can help mitigate financial losses in the event of a security incident.

Board members should also be aware of the potential impact of third-party cyber risk on their company's reputation, financial stability, and compliance obligations. By proactively managing third-party cyber risk, board members can help to protect their company from reputational damage, regulatory penalties, and financial loss.

Legal and Regulatory Considerations in Third-Party Risk Management

A board member plays a critical role in ensuring that their organization complies with legal and regulatory requirements that govern third-party relationships. By taking the following steps, board members can help ensure that their organization is managing third-party risk effectively and avoiding legal and reputational consequences:

1. *Be familiar with the legal and regulatory landscape.* Start by understanding the legal and regulatory requirements that apply to the organization's third-party relationships. These include industry-specific regulations and laws that may require additional security measures for certain data or industries.

2. *Stay informed about changes in the regulatory landscape.* The regulatory landscape is constantly evolving, so it's important to stay informed about changes in the law that may impact the organization's third-party relationships. This may include engaging with legal counsel to understand the potential impact of new or changing laws on the organization's third-party relationships.

3. Ensure that the organization's third-party contracts include clear and enforceable cybersecurity and data protection provisions. These provisions should include requirements for the third party to do the following:
   - Implement appropriate security measures to protect the organization's data.
   - Report any data breaches to the organization promptly.
   - Remediate any security issues identified by the organization.

4. Ensure that the organization has a process to monitor third-party compliance with cybersecurity and data protection requirements. This process should include regular risk assessments, audits, and performance metrics to ensure that third parties meet their contractual obligations and compliance requirements.

Here are some additional tips for board members on legal and regulatory considerations in third-party risk management:

- *Involve legal counsel in the process.* Legal counsel can help board members understand the legal and regulatory landscape and develop and implement appropriate policies and procedures.

- *Make sure third-party contracts are reviewed and approved by the board.* This will help ensure that the contracts include appropriate security and compliance provisions.
- *Conduct regular risk assessments of third-party relationships.* This will help identify and mitigate any risks associated with third-party relationships.
- *Monitor third-party compliance with security and compliance requirements.* This will help ensure that third parties are meeting their obligations and that the organization is protected from security risks.

Sample Questions to ask Third-Party Vendors

The following are some questions a management team or a board may want to ask key third-party vendors:

- What security controls do you have in place to protect our company's sensitive information?
- Have you conducted any security assessments, such as penetration testing or vulnerability scanning, to identify potential weaknesses in your systems?
- Do you have an incident response plan, and have you tested it to ensure its effectiveness?
- How do you monitor for and respond to security incidents or breaches that may impact our company's data?
- How do you ensure that all employees and contractors who have access to our data are properly vetted and trained in security best practices?
- What kind of encryption do you use to protect our data in transit and at rest?
- How do you comply with relevant regulations and industry standards, such as PCI-DSS, HIPAA, and GDPR?
- Have you experienced any security incidents or breaches in the past, and if so, how did you respond to them?

- What kind of insurance coverage do you have in case of a security incident that impacts our company's data?
- Can you provide a copy of your most recent security audit or assessment report?
- What is the scope of your compliance program, and how do you ensure that your organization stays up to date with changing regulatory requirements?
- What specific security measures do you have in place to protect against insider threats and data breaches from within your organization?
- Can you provide documentation or reports to show that your organization has conducted security assessments, penetration testing, or other security audits?
- How do you handle incidents or security breaches, and what is your incident response plan in the event of a breach?
- Can you provide details on your backup and recovery plans, and how quickly can you recover from a major data loss incident?
- What types of third-party security certifications do you have, and can you provide documentation to support these certifications?
- What is your process for monitoring and assessing third-party risks, and how do you ensure that all your vendors and partners follow your organization's security requirements?
- How do you handle security incidents or data breaches that involve your third-party vendors, and what is your process for notifying your customers and stakeholders?
- Can you provide details on your security training programs for employees, and how do you ensure that your staff is aware of and following your organization's security policies?
- How do you handle requests for information or data access from law enforcement or other government

agencies, and what is your process for ensuring that such requests are valid and lawful?

Chapter 7 Summary

This chapter delved into the realm of vendor management and third-party risk in the context of cybersecurity. It highlighted the significance of this topic for board members and provided best practices for effectively managing and mitigating third-party cyber risks.

The chapter emphasized that board members play a crucial role in overseeing cybersecurity efforts, including third-party risk management. By understanding the potential risks associated with third-party relationships, board members can ensure that the organization has appropriate controls to protect sensitive data and critical systems.

To effectively manage third-party cyber risks, the chapter outlined several best practices. It emphasized the importance of implementing a robust vendor management program encompassing due diligence processes, contractual obligations, and ongoing monitoring. Key areas of focus include vendor selection, contract negotiation, security assessments, incident response planning, and termination protocols. By following these best practices, organizations can enhance their resilience to third-party cyber risks and bolster their overall cybersecurity posture.

The chapter highlighted the legal and regulatory considerations involved in third-party risk management. It stressed the need for organizations to align their vendor management practices with applicable laws and regulations to ensure compliance. To aid board members in assessing vendors' cybersecurity capabilities, the chapter provided a set of sample questions that can be asked during vendor evaluations.

In summary, this chapter emphasized the criticality of effective vendor management and third-party risk management in cybersecurity. By actively managing third-party cyber risks, organizations can protect sensitive information, maintain stakeholder trust, and enhance their overall cybersecurity resilience. Board members play a vital role in overseeing these efforts and ensuring the implementation of best practices. Through diligent vendor management, organizations can establish a robust cybersecurity posture that safeguards their digital assets and minimizes potential vulnerabilities.

Chapter 8
Cybersecurity Training and Awareness

In the complex landscape of today's digital world, cybersecurity is no longer a peripheral concern but a central aspect of any organization's operations. This chapter elucidates the integral role of cybersecurity awareness and training in fortifying an organization's defense against cyber threats.

The heart of this chapter is a fundamental principle: cybersecurity is not the exclusive responsibility of the IT department but an organization-wide obligation. Every employee, regardless of their role, contributes to the organization's cyber resilience. Therefore, fostering an awareness of cybersecurity threats and best practices among all employees is not a mere recommendation but a necessity.

As we delve deeper, we will explore the strategies that can be adopted to design and implement robust cybersecurity training and awareness programs. The success of these initiatives hinges on their ability to cater to the distinct needs of an organization and its workforce. Consequently, the strategies discussed will emphasize customization and flexibility, aiming to cultivate a workforce that is not only knowledgeable about cybersecurity but also capable of effectively responding to cyber threats.

Moreover, the chapter will provide a more granular perspective on these training strategies, offering insights into specific techniques that can augment their effectiveness. Whether through traditional seminars, engaging workshops, or innovative simulation exercises, the goal is to equip employees with the necessary skills and knowledge to navigate the evolving landscape of cyber threats.

In essence, this chapter underlines the strategic value of cybersecurity awareness and training, offering board members practical guidance on promoting these initiatives within their organization. By incorporating the insights shared in this chapter, board members can help cultivate a culture of cybersecurity awareness, bolstering the organization's overall cyber resilience.

Cybersecurity Incident: CNA Financial

In March 2021, CNA Financial, a leading U.S. insurance company, suffered a cybersecurity breach that disrupted the company's technology infrastructure and resulted in the theft of company data. The breach, caused by a sophisticated phishing attack, impacted the company's operations, including email systems and customer support services. CNA

(continued)

(continued)

Financial later confirmed that the attackers had stolen some data but did not provide details about the extent of the breach. The company stated that it had launched an investigation into the incident and was working with law enforcement agencies and cybersecurity experts to mitigate the breach's impact. The CNA Financial board of directors would have been responsible for overseeing the company's cybersecurity measures and ensuring that appropriate measures were in place to prevent such an incident.

Importance of Cybersecurity Awareness for All Employees

As cyber threats continue to evolve and grow, it is crucial for businesses to implement comprehensive cybersecurity awareness programs that cover all employees at every level of the organization. Board members play a vital role in ensuring that these programs are in place and effective.

Employees are often the first line of defense against cyberattacks, and their lack of awareness and education can put the entire organization at risk. Most cyberattacks occur due to human error, such as clicking a malicious link or opening a phishing email. Therefore, it is important for board members to understand the importance of cybersecurity awareness training for all employees.

A strong cybersecurity awareness program should be developed with the understanding that all employees, regardless of their position or job function, are potential targets for cyberattacks. The program should be tailored to the specific needs of the organization and should cover topics such as password management, identifying phishing attempts, and safe browsing habits.

Cybersecurity Incident: FACC AG

In 2016, FACC AG, a small Austrian company that supplies parts to aircraft manufacturers, was the victim of a cyberattack that resulted in the loss of more than $50 million. The attackers gained access to the company's financial systems and used fraudulent emails to divert payments to their own accounts.

The attack was a sophisticated spear-phishing campaign that targeted key employees with access to FACC's financial systems. The attackers sent convincing-looking emails that appeared to be from FACC's CEO, requesting a change in bank account details for an existing customer. When the employee made the change, the attackers were able to redirect payments to their own accounts.

The FACC AG board of directors was involved in the aftermath of the attack, and the company faced legal action for the breach. In 2017, FACC AG sued its insurance company for not paying out a claim related to the cyberattack; the insurer cited a lack of proper cybersecurity measures as the reason for the breach.

Board members play a critical role in ensuring that employees receive regular and effective training. This may include reviewing and approving training materials, providing feedback on the program's effectiveness, and ensuring that employees are incentivized to complete the training.

In addition, board members should ensure that the program is up to date with the latest threats and attack methods. This may require working with outside consultants or cybersecurity experts to provide the most effective and current training possible.

By prioritizing cybersecurity awareness and education, board members can help create a culture of security within their organization, reduce the risk of successful cyberattacks, and protect the organization's reputation, finances, and sensitive data.

In the next section, we will discuss strategies for providing effective cybersecurity training and awareness programs to all employees.

Strategies for Providing Effective Training and Awareness Programs

Board members play a critical role in ensuring that their organization has an effective training and awareness program. By taking the following steps, board members can help to ensure that their organization is prepared to defend against cyberattacks:

1. *Understand the importance of training and awareness.* Training and awareness programs are essential for creating a culture of cybersecurity within the organization. By educating employees about the latest cyber threats and attack techniques, board members can help them identify and respond to potential threats.

2. *Get buy-in from senior management.* Training and awareness programs are most effective when they have the support of senior management. Work with the CEO and other senior leaders to ensure that they are committed to the program and willing to allocate the necessary resources.

3. *Develop a comprehensive program.* The organization's training and awareness program should be comprehensive and tailored to the specific needs of the organization. It should cover a variety of topics, including the following:
   - Basic cyber hygiene practices, such as password management and safe browsing habits
   - Social engineering awareness
   - The latest cyber threats and attack techniques
   - Best practices for identifying and responding to potential threats

4. *Make the program engaging and interactive.* Employees are more likely to remember information they learn in a fun and engaging way. Use a variety of teaching methods, such as lectures, simulations, and games, to keep employees' attention.

5. *Measure the program's effectiveness.* It is important to measure the effectiveness of the training and awareness program to ensure that it is meeting its goals. Board members can do this by surveying employees to assess their knowledge and skills or tracking the number of cyber incidents that occur.

6. *Update the program regularly.* The cyber threat landscape is constantly evolving, so it is important to update the training and awareness program regularly to reflect the latest threats and risks.

In addition to these steps, board members can play a crucial role in ensuring the effectiveness of their organization's training and awareness program by implementing the following strategies. First, involving employees in the development of the program can significantly enhance engagement and participation. By forming a committee comprising employees from different departments, organizations can gain valuable insights and perspectives that contribute to the program's design and delivery. This collaborative approach fosters a sense of ownership and relevance among employees.

Second, tailoring the program to employees' specific job roles and responsibilities is essential. When training content aligns with their day-to-day work, employees are more likely to pay attention and apply the knowledge gained. By customizing the training materials and activities to address the unique needs and challenges of different roles, organizations can ensure maximum relevance and impact.

Third, making the program accessible to all employees is crucial for its success. Providing various formats, such as online modules, in-person sessions, and self-paced resources, allows individuals to choose the most convenient and effective learning method based on their preferences and work environments. This inclusivity ensures that all employees, regardless of their location or work style, have equal opportunities to participate and benefit from the training.

Finally, recognizing the need for ongoing training and refreshers is vital. Knowledge and skills can quickly become outdated in the rapidly evolving cybersecurity landscape. Board members should advocate for regular training updates and refreshers to keep employees informed and equipped with the latest cybersecurity practices. This can be accomplished through channels such as newsletters, webinars, or online resources that provide continuous learning opportunities and reinforce the importance of cybersecurity awareness.

By implementing these strategies, board members can actively contribute to the success of their organization's training and awareness program, ensuring that it effectively reaches and educates all employees.

More Detail on Effective Training Strategies

When it comes to cybersecurity training, organizations need to go beyond basic awareness and provide employees with practical skills and knowledge to defend against cyber threats. Here are some additional strategies to enhance the effectiveness of cybersecurity training programs:

- *Real-world scenarios*: Instead of relying solely on theoretical content, incorporating simulated real-world scenarios can help employees understand how cyber threats manifest in their daily work environment. Interactive exercises, such as tabletop simulations or red team/blue team exercises, allow employees to apply their knowledge in a practical setting and make informed decisions to mitigate risks.
- *Role-based training*: Recognize that different roles within the organization have distinct cybersecurity responsibilities. Tailor training programs to address the specific needs and risks associated with each role. For example, IT administrators may require training on network security and system vulnerabilities, while nontechnical staff can benefit from guidance on email phishing and secure browsing practices. Customizing the training content ensures relevance and increases the likelihood of adoption.
- *Gamification and microlearning*: Engage employees through gamification techniques and microlearning modules. Gamification elements, such as leaderboards, badges, and rewards, create a sense of competition and

motivate employees to actively participate in training activities. Microlearning breaks down complex topics into bite-sized modules that can be completed quickly, making it easier for employees to fit training into their busy schedules and retain information effectively.

- *Continuous reinforcement*: Cybersecurity threats evolve rapidly, making it crucial to provide ongoing reinforcement of training concepts. Regularly reinforce key cybersecurity principles through email reminders, posters, or short quizzes. This helps reinforce learning, keeps cybersecurity top of mind, and encourages a culture of security awareness throughout the organization.
- *Measure and assess*: Establish metrics to assess the effectiveness of cybersecurity training programs. This could include tracking completion rates, analyzing user feedback, or conducting simulated phishing campaigns to gauge employees' susceptibility to social engineering attacks. Regular assessments provide insights into the program's strengths and areas for improvement, allowing organizations to refine their training strategies accordingly.
- *Leadership support and communication*: Strong leadership support is essential for the success of cybersecurity training initiatives. Executives should lead by example and actively promote a culture of security awareness within the organization. Clear and consistent communication about the importance of cybersecurity, the potential risks, and the role employees play in protecting sensitive information can significantly reinforce the training message.

By implementing these additional strategies, organizations can take their cybersecurity training programs to the next level, empowering employees with practical skills and fostering a security-conscious culture. Remember, cybersecurity is a shared responsibility, and ongoing training is essential to stay ahead of evolving threats in the digital landscape.

Chapter 8 Summary

This chapter emphasized that cybersecurity is an organization-wide responsibility, not just an IT concern. The importance of fostering cybersecurity awareness among all employees was underscored as a necessity rather than an option, given the interconnected nature of today's digital work environments.

We delved into effective strategies for designing and implementing cybersecurity training and awareness programs, highlighting the significance of customization and adaptability to the unique needs of an organization and its workforce. From traditional educational methods to interactive simulations, a variety of approaches were examined to equip employees with the necessary knowledge and skills to counter cyber threats.

In a more detailed segment, we analyzed these training strategies, providing board members with practical insights into how they can enhance the effectiveness of these programs within their organizations. The objective remains to cultivate a workforce that is not only aware of cybersecurity risks but also proficient in responding to them.

Ultimately, the chapter underscored the strategic value of comprehensive cybersecurity training and awareness programs. It offered board members a road map to effectively promote these initiatives within their organizations, thereby fostering a robust culture of cybersecurity awareness. This culture, in turn, significantly bolsters an organization's resilience against cyber threats and ensures continuity in an ever-evolving digital landscape.

Chapter 9
Cyber Insurance

As previously discussed, cyberattacks, such as data breaches, ransomware attacks, and phishing scams, have grown in frequency and sophistication, making them a significant concern for businesses worldwide. These attacks can result in devastating financial losses, operational disruptions, and reputational damage, necessitating a robust risk management strategy. A key component of this strategy is cyber insurance.

Cyber insurance offers businesses a financial safety net, helping them cope with the adverse effects of cyber incidents. It is specifically designed to address the unique risks associated with cyber threats, offering coverage for a broad range of losses and expenses that a business may incur due to a cyber incident. These can include costs related to business interruption, data recovery, legal and public relations expenses, customer notifications, credit monitoring, and, in certain circumstances, even extortion payments.

As the threat landscape continues to evolve, cyber insurance has become a crucial consideration for board members. They must understand its nuances to make informed decisions about the policy that best fits their organization's risk profile and budget. This chapter aims to provide board members with a comprehensive understanding of cyber insurance, exploring its key components, coverage options, cost factors, and best practices for policy management.

Understanding Cyber Insurance

What Is Cyber Insurance?

Cyber insurance, also known as *cyber risk insurance* or *cyber liability insurance*, is a form of coverage designed to protect businesses from Internet-based risks and, more generally, risks related to information technology infrastructure and activities. It is intended to mitigate losses from various cyber incidents, including data breaches, business interruption, and network damage.

Cyber insurance policies can be structured to cover a variety of costs associated with a cyber incident, depending on the specific needs of the organization. These may include costs associated with the following:

- *Business interruption*: Covers the loss of income a business suffers after a cyberattack disrupts its normal business operations
- *Data loss and recovery*: Covers the costs of recovering lost or compromised data and repairing damaged systems and networks
- *Notification and credit monitoring*: Covers the costs of notifying affected customers and providing credit monitoring services in the event of a data breach
- *Legal fees and liability*: Covers the legal costs associated with lawsuits and other legal actions resulting from a cyber incident
- *Public relations*: Covers the costs of managing the company's public image and reputation after a cyber incident

- *Extortion payments*: Covers the costs associated with responding to a ransomware attack, including potential payment of the ransom demand

While cyber insurance can offer critical financial protection in the event of a cyber incident, it's crucial to understand that it is not a substitute for robust cybersecurity measures. Implementing proactive security measures and maintaining a robust cybersecurity posture remains essential to prevent cyber incidents and reduce the potential damage if an incident does occur.

Why Is Cyber Insurance Important?

In the digital era, businesses depend heavily on information technology for their operations. This dependence, coupled with the rise in cyber threats, means businesses of all sizes and across all sectors are at risk of cyberattacks. The potential financial impact of these attacks can be crippling. A report by Cybersecurity Ventures predicts that by 2025, cybercrime will cost the world $10.5 trillion annually, up from $3 trillion in 2015.

However, the financial implications of a cyber incident extend beyond the immediate costs of responding to the incident. Businesses also need to consider the potential loss of customer trust, damage to their reputation, and loss of intellectual property. These indirect costs can often exceed the immediate response costs and have long-term implications for the business's viability.

This is where cyber insurance comes in. By providing financial support in the aftermath of a cyber incident, it can help businesses weather the storm and recover more quickly. It can also provide businesses access to expert resources, such as legal professionals, public relations consultants, and cybersecurity experts, to help manage the incident and mitigate its impact.

Evolution of Cyber Insurance

Cyber insurance is a relatively new form of coverage that emerged in the late 1990s due to the growing dependence on technology and the Internet. The first cyber insurance policies were relatively simple, providing coverage for liability arising from website content and some limited forms of data-breach liability. However, as the cyber threat landscape evolved, so did cyber insurance.

Over the past two decades, cyber insurance policies have become more complex and nuanced, offering coverage for a wide range of cyber risks. The sophistication of these policies has evolved in tandem with the increasing complexity of cyber threats, the growing regulatory landscape around data privacy and protection, and the realization of the potentially catastrophic impact of cyber incidents on businesses.

Today, cyber insurance is considered an essential part of a comprehensive risk management strategy for businesses of all sizes and across all sectors. It provides not just financial protection but also a valuable resource for navigating the complex aftermath of a cyber incident.

The Role of the Board in Cyber Insurance

The board plays a crucial role in an organization's cyber insurance decisions. As the custodians of the organization's strategic direction and risk management, board members need to understand the potential impact of cyber risks on the organization and ensure that the organization has adequate coverage to protect against these risks.

The board's role in cyber insurance includes doing the following:

- *Setting the organization's risk appetite*: The board needs to establish the organization's risk tolerance level, which will guide decisions about the type and amount of cyber insurance coverage needed.

- *Understanding the organization's cyber risk profile*: This involves understanding the types of cyber risks the organization faces, the potential impact of these risks, and how these risks are being managed.
- *Ensuring alignment with the organization's risk management strategy*: The board needs to ensure that the cyber insurance coverage aligns with and complements the organization's overall risk management strategy.
- *Overseeing the cyber insurance purchase process*: This includes reviewing and approving the cyber insurance policy, ensuring that it provides adequate coverage, and is priced appropriately.
- *Ensuring compliance with cyber insurance policy requirements*: The board needs to ensure that the organization complies with the terms and conditions of the policy, including any cybersecurity measures the insurer requires the organization to implement.

Key Components of Cyber Insurance

In this section, we delve into the intricacies of cyber insurance policies, highlighting their key components and nuances. Understanding these elements will enable board members to assess the suitability of a policy and make informed decisions that align with the organization's risk management strategy.

Types of Coverage

Cyber insurance policies provide two main types of coverage: first-party coverage and third-party coverage.

First-party coverage protects the policyholder against losses incurred directly by the organization due to a cyber incident. These can include costs related to business interruption, data recovery, public relations efforts, and customer notification and credit monitoring. Some policies may also cover the costs of ransom payments in response to a ransomware attack.

Third-party coverage protects the policyholder against claims made by others as a result of a cyber incident. These can include legal defense costs, settlements, and judgments related to lawsuits filed against the organization due to a data breach or other cyber incident.

While most cyber insurance policies offer both first-party and third-party coverage, the specific coverage terms and limits can vary significantly between policies. It's therefore crucial for board members to understand these differences and assess which types of coverage are most relevant to their organization's risk profile.

Policy Limits and Deductibles

As with any insurance policy, cyber insurance policies have policy limits and deductibles that board members need to understand. The *policy limit* is the maximum amount the insurer will pay out for a covered loss, while the *deductible* is the amount the policyholder must pay out of pocket before the insurer will start to pay.

Policy limits can vary significantly depending on the size and risk profile of the organization, as well as the specific terms of the policy. Some policies may also have sublimits for specific types of coverage, such as business interruption or data recovery.

The deductible can also vary and is typically set based on the organization's risk tolerance and budget. Higher deductibles can result in lower premium costs but can also increase the organization's financial burden in the event of a claim.

Exclusions

Exclusions are specific situations or circumstances not covered by the insurance policy. In the context of cyber insurance, common exclusions may include losses caused by

- War or terrorism
- Criminal or fraudulent acts by the policyholder
- Unencrypted data
- Failure to maintain or update security measures
- Acts of God, such as earthquakes or floods

Understanding these exclusions is crucial, as they can significantly impact the extent of coverage provided by the policy. Board members need to review these exclusions carefully and assess their relevance to the organization's risk profile. In some cases, it may be possible to negotiate with the insurer to remove or modify certain exclusions.

Retroactive Dates

Retroactive dates are a common feature in cyber insurance policies and represent the date after which the insurer will cover claims. The policy will not cover any cyber incidents that occur before this date.

This is particularly important for cyber insurance because cyber incidents, especially data breaches, can take a long time to discover. According to a 2020 report by IBM, the average time to identify a breach was 207 days. This means a breach could occur before the retroactive date but not be discovered until after the policy is in force. In this situation, the insurer would not cover the claim.

Therefore, board members need to be aware of the retroactive date in their organization's cyber insurance policy and understand its implications. In some cases, it may be possible to negotiate a retroactive date that provides more comprehensive coverage.

Policy Periods

The *policy period* is the length of time during which the insurance coverage is in effect. For most insurance policies, this is typically one year, but it can be longer or shorter depending on the policy's specific terms.

During the policy period, the insurer will cover any claims resulting from cyber incidents that occur during this time and are reported to the insurer. However, claims related to incidents that occur outside the policy period, even if they are reported during the policy period, may not be covered. This is known as the "claims-made" basis of coverage, which is common in cyber insurance policies.

This makes it crucial for board members to ensure that the organization promptly reports any potential cyber incidents to the insurer. Failure to do so could result in the insurer denying the claim.

Cyber Risk Assessments

Many insurers require policyholders to undergo a cyber risk assessment as part of the underwriting process. This assessment involves an evaluation of the organization's cybersecurity posture, including its security policies and procedures, network and system security measures, incident response plans, and employee training programs.

The results of the cyber risk assessment can significantly affect the cost and terms of the policy. For instance, organizations with robust cybersecurity measures and a strong culture of security awareness may be able to secure more favorable terms and lower premiums.

Board members should ensure that the organization is well-prepared for the cyber risk assessment and that it accurately reflects the organization's cybersecurity practices. They should also consider using the results of the assessment as a benchmark to improve the organization's cybersecurity posture.

Evaluating and Purchasing Cyber Insurance

In this section, we explore the process of evaluating and purchasing cyber insurance. We provide guidance on assessing an organization's risk profile, determining the appropriate coverage level, and selecting the right insurer.

Assessing the Organization's Risk Profile

The first step in purchasing cyber insurance is to assess the organization's risk profile. This involves identifying the cyber threats the organization is most likely to face and estimating the potential impact of these threats on the organization. Board members should consider factors such as these:

- *The nature of the organization's business*: Certain industries, such as healthcare and financial services, are more likely to be targeted by cyberattacks due to the sensitive data they handle.
- *The organization's use of technology*: Organizations that rely heavily on digital technologies for their operations may be more at risk of cyber incidents.
- *The organization's data practices*: Organizations that collect and store large amounts of sensitive data may face a higher risk of data breaches.
- *The organization's regulatory environment*: Organizations subject to stringent data protection regulations

may face additional risks, such as fines and penalties for noncompliance.

This risk assessment can help board members determine the types of coverage the organization needs and the appropriate policy limits. It can also guide them in selecting an insurer that has expertise in covering the specific risks the organization faces.

Determining the Appropriate Level of Coverage

Determining the appropriate level of coverage is a complex task that requires a careful analysis of the organization's risk profile and financial resources. The goal is to strike a balance between the cost of the insurance and the potential financial impact of a cyber incident. Board members should consider factors such as the following:

- *The potential costs of a cyber incident*: These include direct costs, such as business interruption, data recovery, and legal fees, as well as indirect costs, such as reputational damage and loss of customer trust.
- *The organization's financial resources*: Organizations with limited financial resources may need more extensive coverage to ensure that they can cope with the financial impact of a cyber incident.
- *The organization's risk tolerance*: Organizations with a high risk tolerance may be willing to accept a higher deductible or lower policy limits in exchange for lower premiums.

Board members may wish to consult with a broker or insurance advisor to help them determine the appropriate level of coverage. These professionals have the expertise to assess the organization's risk profile, understand the nuances of cyber insurance policies, and negotiate favorable terms with insurers.

Selecting an Insurer

Selecting an insurer is a critical decision that can significantly impact the effectiveness of the organization's cyber insurance coverage. Board members should consider factors such as these:

- *The insurer's financial strength*: The insurer should have the financial resources to pay out claims, especially in the event of a large-scale cyber incident.
- *The insurer's reputation*: The insurer should have a good reputation for handling claims fairly and promptly.
- *The insurer's expertise in cyber insurance*: The insurer should have a deep understanding of cyber risks and the ability to offer coverage that meets the organization's specific needs.
- *The insurer's customer service*: The insurer should offer excellent customer service, including prompt and responsive claims handling and access to expert resources.

Insurance brokers can provide insight into the insurer's financial strength, reputation, and customer service and negotiate favorable terms on the organization's behalf.

Negotiating Terms and Conditions

Once the organization has selected an insurer, the next step is to negotiate the terms and conditions of the policy. This involves discussing the organization's needs and concerns with the insurer and reaching an agreement on the policy's details, including coverages, policy limits, deductibles, and exclusions.

Board members should actively participate in this process to ensure that the policy meets the organization's needs. They should work with the insurer (or a broker or insurance advisor, if one is involved) to understand the policy's details and negotiate changes, if necessary. Key areas to focus on include the following:

- *Coverage*: Ensure that the policy covers the types of cyber incidents the organization is most likely to face, such as data breaches, ransomware attacks, and business interruption incidents.
- *Policy limits*: Determine whether the policy limits are sufficient to cover the potential financial impact of a cyber incident.
- *Deductibles*: Consider whether the organization can afford to pay the deductible out of pocket in the event of a claim.
- *Exclusions*: Review the policy's exclusions carefully, and assess whether they leave any significant gaps in coverage. If so, try to negotiate with the insurer to remove or modify these exclusions.
- *Retroactive dates*: If the policy includes a retroactive date, consider whether this date provides sufficient coverage. If not, try to negotiate a more favorable date.

During the negotiation process, board members should be prepared to provide the insurer with detailed information about the organization's risk profile and cybersecurity practices. This can help the insurer understand the organization's needs and offer a policy that meets these needs.

Implementing the Policy

Once the organization has purchased a cyber insurance policy, the next step is to implement the policy. This involves communicating the policy's details to relevant stakeholders, integrating the policy into the organization's risk management processes, and ensuring that the organization complies with the policy's conditions. Key steps in this process include the following:

- *Communicating the policy*: Inform relevant stakeholders, such as employees, customers, and partners, about the policy. This can help them understand how the policy affects them and what they need to do to comply with its conditions.
- *Integrating the policy*: Incorporate the policy into the organization's risk management processes. For instance, the organization's incident response plan should include steps for reporting a cyber incident to the insurer.
- *Complying with the policy*: Ensure that the organization complies with the policy's conditions, such as maintaining adequate security measures and promptly reporting cyber incidents. Failure to comply with these conditions could result in the insurer denying a claim.

Managing and Reviewing the Cyber Insurance Policy

In this section, we explore how to manage and review a cyber insurance policy. We discuss how to file a claim, manage a claim dispute, and review and renew the policy.

Filing a Claim

If the organization experiences a cyber incident, it will need to file a claim with the insurer. This process typically involves notifying the insurer about the incident, providing the insurer with information about the incident and its impact, and working with the insurer to resolve the claim. Key steps in this process include the following:

- *Notifying the insurer*: Notify the insurer of the incident as soon as possible. Most cyber insurance policies require policyholders to report incidents promptly, so it's important to act quickly.

- *Documenting the incident*: Document the incident and its impact in detail. This should include information about the nature of the incident, the extent of the damage, the steps taken to respond to the incident, and the costs incurred as a result of the incident.
- *Cooperating with the insurer*: Cooperate with the insurer during the claims process. This may involve providing additional information, participating in investigations, and complying with the insurer's requests.

During the claims process, it's important to maintain regular communication with the insurer and to be honest and forthcoming about the incident and its impact. This can help ensure a smooth and successful claims process.

Managing a Claim Dispute

In some cases, the organization may disagree with the insurer's handling of a claim. This could involve a disagreement over the cause of the incident, the extent of the damage, or the amount of the claim payout.

If this happens, the organization should first try to resolve the dispute with the insurer. This involves discussing the issue with the insurer, providing additional evidence or arguments, and negotiating a resolution.

If the dispute cannot be resolved through negotiation, the organization may need to consider other options, such as mediation or arbitration. In some cases, it may be necessary to take legal action against the insurer. However, this should be a last resort, as it can be costly and time-consuming.

Reviewing and Renewing the Policy

Cyber risks are constantly evolving, so it's important for organizations to regularly review and update their cyber insurance policies. This involves assessing the policy's effectiveness, identifying gaps in coverage, and negotiating updates with the insurer. These are the key steps in this process:

- *Assessing the policy*: Evaluate the policy's effectiveness in covering the organization's cyber risks. This could involve reviewing the organization's claims history, analyzing recent cyber incidents, and getting feedback from stakeholders.
- *Identifying gaps*: Identify any gaps in coverage that have emerged since the policy was purchased. They could be due to changes in the organization's risk profile, changes in the cyber risk landscape, or shortcomings in the policy itself.
- *Negotiating updates*: Discuss any necessary updates with the insurer. This could involve increasing the policy limits, expanding the coverages, adjusting the deductibles, or modifying the exclusions.

When renewing the policy, the organization should also consider whether it's worth switching to a different insurer. This could be due to dissatisfaction with the current insurer, a better offer from a different insurer, or changes in the organization's needs or circumstances.

Chapter 9 Summary

This chapter provided a comprehensive exploration of the role of cyber insurance in managing cyber risks, outlining the importance of insurance in a broader cybersecurity strategy and highlighting the process of selecting, purchasing, implementing, managing, and renewing a cyber insurance policy. Given the escalating threat landscape and potential financial implications of cyber incidents, we began by highlighting the increasing importance of cyber insurance as an integral part of a broader cybersecurity risk management strategy. Cyber insurance transfers some of the financial risks associated with cyber incidents to a third party, complementing other risk management measures, such as preventive security controls and incident response plans.

The chapter also detailed the process of choosing a suitable cyber insurance policy. This process requires a detailed risk assessment to understand the organization's specific cyber risks and identify the ideal policy requirements. It is crucial to involve all relevant stakeholders in the decision-making process, including board members, management, IT staff, and legal counsel, to ensure that the selected policy aligns with the organization's needs and risk tolerance.

Negotiating the terms and conditions of a policy was also covered, emphasizing the need for clarity and precision in certain areas, such as coverage, policy limits, deductibles, exclusions, and retroactive dates. Board members should ensure that the policy covers potential cyber incidents sufficiently, and they should fully understand the policy's terms to avoid future complications.

Policy implementation was then discussed, including communication with stakeholders, integration into risk management processes, and compliance with policy conditions. This step is crucial for the smooth operation of the policy and the success of any future claims.

The chapter also dealt with the practicalities of managing a policy, including filing a claim and handling claim disputes. The emphasis was on maintaining open and honest communication with the insurer, documenting incidents thoroughly, and being cooperative during the claims process. Dispute resolution strategies were suggested, with legal action recommended as a last resort.

Finally, the chapter stressed the importance of regularly reviewing and updating the cyber insurance policy, considering the rapidly evolving nature of cyber threats. Organizations should evaluate their policy's effectiveness, identify coverage gaps, and negotiate necessary updates with the insurer.

While cyber insurance is a vital tool for managing cyber risks, it must be complemented by proactive cybersecurity measures. By understanding the intricacies of cyber insurance, board members can help their organization stay resilient in the face of escalating cyber threats.

Chapter 10
Conclusion: Moving Forward with Cybersecurity Governance

As we conclude this book, it is crucial to emphasize that cybersecurity governance is an ongoing journey that requires continuous attention and dedication. The rapidly evolving threat landscape demands constant adaptation and vigilance to effectively protect organizations from cyber risks. This is particularly significant for small and medium-sized businesses that may face greater vulnerabilities due to limited resources and expertise in cybersecurity.

Throughout this book, we have explored the pivotal role of cybersecurity governance and the responsibilities of board members in ensuring the adequate protection of their company. As we look ahead, let us reflect on the key takeaways from our discussions and provide actionable steps for board members to consider as they advance their cybersecurity governance efforts.

First, it is vital for board members to recognize the criticality of cybersecurity governance within the overall corporate governance framework. Establishing a cybersecurity culture from the top down and developing a comprehensive cybersecurity strategy aligned with the organization's goals are foundational steps.

Understanding the organization's unique cyber risks and engaging with cybersecurity experts are crucial components of effective cybersecurity governance. Board members must oversee the establishment of robust risk management processes and frameworks to mitigate cyber threats.

Ensuring cybersecurity awareness and education for both board members and employees is essential. Ongoing training programs that enhance cyber literacy and foster a security-conscious culture throughout the organization are key to minimizing risks.

Third-party risk management is another critical aspect of cybersecurity governance. Board members must ensure that appropriate due diligence is conducted on vendors and partners and that contractual agreements include robust cybersecurity requirements.

Preparing and regularly testing an incident response plan is vital for minimizing the impact of cyber incidents. Board members should oversee the development and implementation of effective incident response strategies to facilitate swift recovery.

Engaging in independent cybersecurity audits and assessments provides valuable insights into the organization's security posture. Board members should support these audits and use the findings to identify areas for improvement.

Allocating adequate resources and budgeting for cybersecurity are paramount. Board members must prioritize cybersecurity investments to implement and maintain effective security measures.

Cybersecurity Incident: Facebook/Cambridge Analytica

In 2018, Facebook was embroiled in a scandal involving the misuse of personal data from millions of Facebook users by the political consulting firm Cambridge Analytica. The data was collected through a third-party app, which harvested information from users' profiles without their knowledge or consent.

Cambridge Analytica used the data to build psychological profiles of voters in the 2016 U.S. Presidential election, which it used to target political ads to specific groups of voters. The scandal sparked widespread public outcry and scrutiny of Facebook's data privacy practices.

Facebook's board of directors was heavily involved in the aftermath of the scandal, and the company faced legal action and regulatory scrutiny for the data breach. The company's CEO, Mark Zuckerberg, was called to testify before the U.S. Congress and the European Parliament, and the company faced significant reputational damage as a result of the scandal.

The incident led to a shakeup of Facebook's board of directors, with several directors stepping down and new members being appointed to oversee the company's data privacy and security practices. The board also established a committee to review the company's data privacy policies and made

(continued)

(continued)

significant changes to its platform to give users more control over their personal data.

The Facebook/Cambridge Analytica scandal highlighted the need for companies to take data privacy seriously and implement robust measures to protect user data. It also underscored the role that boards of directors play in overseeing and holding executives accountable for the company's data privacy practices. Companies should regularly review their data privacy policies and security measures and provide transparency to users about how their data is collected and used. Additionally, boards should have a clear understanding of the company's data privacy practices and ensure that the company is taking sufficient steps to protect user data from potential misuse or breaches.

Establishing key performance indicators (KPIs) and implementing regular reporting mechanisms are vital for assessing the effectiveness of cybersecurity measures. Board members should monitor these metrics to gauge the organization's cyber risk posture.

Understanding the potential benefits and limitations of cyber insurance is crucial. Board members should collaborate with management and insurance brokers to ensure appropriate coverage that aligns with the organization's specific risks.

The Board's Role in Cybersecurity Governance

It is evident that the board's role in cybersecurity governance is of paramount importance. In this section, we will delve deeper into the specific responsibilities of board members and the key considerations they should keep in mind when overseeing their organization's cybersecurity efforts.

First, it is crucial for board members to recognize that cybersecurity is not solely the responsibility of the IT department or designated cybersecurity teams. Instead, it is a collective responsibility that should be embraced by every member of the organization, starting from the board itself. By setting the tone at the top, board members can establish a culture of cybersecurity awareness and diligence throughout the organization.

The board plays a vital role in shaping the organization's cybersecurity posture by providing strategic direction and guidance. Board members should work closely with management to establish clear expectations and goals for cybersecurity, ensuring that it aligns with the organization's overall mission and objectives. This involves setting the right tone, emphasizing the importance of cybersecurity, and integrating it into the organization's risk management framework.

To effectively oversee cybersecurity governance, board members must possess a comprehensive understanding of the specific risks and threats facing the organization. This includes staying informed about emerging cybersecurity trends, regulatory requirements, and industry best practices. By regularly engaging with cybersecurity experts and staying abreast of the evolving landscape, board members can make informed decisions and provide valuable insights to the organization.

One of the key responsibilities of the board is to review and assess the organization's cybersecurity posture on an ongoing basis. This involves evaluating the effectiveness of existing cybersecurity measures, identifying vulnerabilities, and determining the adequacy of resources allocated to cybersecurity initiatives. Board members should work collaboratively with management to establish robust reporting mechanisms that provide transparency and visibility into the organization's cybersecurity performance.

In addition to assessing the current state of cybersecurity, the board must play an active role in developing and implementing strategies to enhance the organization's cyber resilience. This includes working with management to prioritize cybersecurity investments, establish appropriate risk mitigation measures, and ensure the organization's ability to respond effectively to cyber incidents. The board should also advocate for regular cybersecurity training and awareness programs to ensure that employees at all levels are equipped with the necessary knowledge and skills to safeguard the organization's assets.

Board members should regularly evaluate the organization's cybersecurity governance framework to ensure its effectiveness. This involves reviewing policies, procedures, and controls and identifying opportunities for improvement. By conducting periodic assessments and independent audits, board members can gain insights into the organization's cybersecurity strengths and weaknesses, enabling them to make informed decisions about allocating resources and prioritizing initiatives.

As the threat landscape evolves, board members must remain vigilant and proactive in addressing cybersecurity risks. This includes staying informed about emerging threats and technological advancements, as well as using external expertise and collaborating with industry peers to share insights and best practices.

The board's role in cybersecurity governance is crucial for ensuring the organization's resilience in the face of cyber threats. By setting the tone, providing strategic direction, and overseeing the organization's cybersecurity efforts, board members can create a culture of cybersecurity awareness and position the organization for success in an increasingly digital and interconnected world.

Key Takeaways and Action Items for Board Members

As a board member, it is important to understand the significant role that cybersecurity governance plays in ensuring the protection of the organization's data, reputation, and overall operations. Throughout this book, we have covered a variety of topics that are crucial for any board member to know to oversee cybersecurity effectively. Here are the key takeaways and action items for board members:

- *Make cybersecurity a top priority.* Cybersecurity should be a key item on the agenda for every board meeting. Board members should ensure that the necessary resources are allocated to keep the company's cyber defenses up to date and that management is held accountable for maintaining a strong cybersecurity posture.
- *Develop a clear cybersecurity governance framework.* A well-defined cybersecurity governance framework should be in place to ensure that all aspects of cybersecurity are covered. The framework should be reviewed periodically to ensure that it is up to date and relevant.
- *Understand the company's cyber risk profile.* Board members should be aware of the company's cyber risk profile and ensure that appropriate controls are in place to mitigate those risks.
- *Prioritize cybersecurity awareness and training.* Employee education and training are key to ensuring that everyone in the organization knows their role in maintaining a strong cybersecurity posture. Board members should ensure that the necessary resources are allocated for this purpose.
- *Conduct regular assessments and testing.* Regular assessments are critical to identifying vulnerabilities and weaknesses in the organization's cybersecurity posture.

Board members should ensure that such testing is conducted periodically and that the results are used to make necessary improvements.

- *Stay current on legal and regulatory requirements.* Cybersecurity regulations and laws constantly evolve. Board members should stay current on these requirements to ensure that the organization is in compliance and that appropriate measures are taken to address any new or emerging risks.
- *Ensure proper vendor management.* Third-party vendors and service providers can pose a significant risk to the organization. Board members should ensure that the organization's vendor management program is robust and that all third-party risks are identified and mitigated.

By following these key takeaways and action items, board members can play an active role in maintaining a strong cybersecurity posture for their organization. Remember, cybersecurity is not just an IT issue; it is a business issue that requires the attention and oversight of the entire board.

Chapter 10 Summary

We concluded our comprehensive exploration of cybersecurity governance in this final chapter, reaffirming its enduring relevance and the vital role of board members in protecting organizations from cyber threats. Throughout our discourse, we underscored the duties and contemplations board members should undertake to ensure a robust cybersecurity governance framework.

This concluding chapter provided a retrospective on the salient points from our conversations and outlined practical guidelines for board members to further their cybersecurity governance initiatives.

Board members are entrusted with the significant responsibility of establishing a cybersecurity culture and strategy that is in alignment with the organization's objectives. They must demonstrate a keen understanding and management of cyber risks, engage meaningfully with cybersecurity professionals, and facilitate the inception of solid risk management processes.

The emphasis on cybersecurity consciousness and education for board members and employees alike cannot be overstated. Continual training initiatives that nurture a security-aware culture can significantly mitigate risks. Third-party risk management should be high on the board's priority list, involving rigorous due diligence of vendors and partners and the inclusion of cybersecurity provisions in contracts.

A well-structured incident response plan is a cornerstone for rapid recovery from cyber incidents, and the development and execution of the plan should be overseen by the board. Independent cybersecurity audits and evaluations can offer insightful revelations, pinpointing areas that require enhancement.

The allocation of adequate resources and budget for cybersecurity is of utmost importance. Board members should advocate for investments in cybersecurity to implement and sustain effective protective measures. The establishment of KPIs and frequent reporting mechanisms facilitates the continuous evaluation of cybersecurity effectiveness.

Comprehending the advantages and constraints of cyber insurance is also critical. Board members should work in tandem with management and insurance brokers to ensure coverage that aligns with the specific risks faced by the organization.

In summary, this chapter reiterated the continuous nature of cybersecurity governance and the critical role of board members. By adopting the key takeaways and implementing the suggested steps, board members can efficiently safeguard their organizations from cyber threats, ensuring resilience and upholding stakeholder trust in an increasingly digital world.

Appendix A

Checklist of Key Considerations for Board Members

Here is a checklist of key considerations for board members around cybersecurity:

- Understanding key cybersecurity concepts and terminology
- Recognizing common cyber threats and risks faced by companies
- Familiarizing themselves with relevant cybersecurity regulations and laws
- Developing an effective cybersecurity governance framework
- Engaging in regular reporting and executive briefings on cybersecurity issues
- Conducting regular cybersecurity risk assessments
- Implementing strategies for managing third-party risk

- Providing effective cybersecurity training and awareness programs for all employees
- Understanding cyber insurance and considering coverage options
- Maintaining a culture of cybersecurity awareness and vigilance across the organization

Board members should work closely with senior management and IT teams to ensure that these considerations are integrated into the company's overall risk management framework. By taking a proactive approach to cybersecurity governance, board members can help protect their organization against cyber threats and reduce the risk of reputational damage, financial loss, and legal liability.

Appendix B

Sample Questions

Here are some examples of questions that board members could ask the management team in regard to cybersecurity:

- What are the most critical cybersecurity risks the organization is facing?
- How is the organization currently addressing cybersecurity risks?
- What is the current cybersecurity posture of the organization, and how is it being measured?
- Has the organization conducted a recent cybersecurity risk assessment?
- What is the incident response plan for a cybersecurity breach, and has it been tested?
- How is the organization updated on the latest cybersecurity threats and vulnerabilities?
- Is the organization compliant with all relevant cybersecurity regulations and standards?
- How does the organization ensure that all employees are trained in cybersecurity best practices?

- Does the organization have a cybersecurity insurance policy, and what does it cover?
- How is the organization managing third-party vendor cybersecurity risks?

Appendix C

Sample Board Meeting Agenda

H ere's a sample board meeting agenda focused on cybersecurity:

1. Cybersecurity risk management report
   a) Presentation of current cybersecurity risk posture
   b) Discussion of new and emerging cyber threats
   c) Review of ongoing cybersecurity initiatives and progress
2. Executive session for confidential cybersecurity matters
3. Third-party risk management report
   a) Overview of the third-party risk management program
   b) Discussion of key third-party risks and mitigating controls
   c) Review of vendor cybersecurity assessments and risk ratings
4. Cybersecurity training and awareness report
   a) Update on employee cybersecurity training program
   b) Review of cybersecurity awareness campaigns and initiatives

5. Legal and regulatory compliance report
   a) Overview of applicable cybersecurity regulations and laws
   b) Discussion of compliance status and progress
   c) Review of industry standards and best practices
6. Cyber incident response report
   a) Review of the incident response plan
   b) Discussion of recent cyber incidents and lessons learned

Note that the agenda can be adjusted to fit the organization's and the board's specific needs.

Appendix D
List of Key Vendors

The following are key vendor types that a company may consider engaging for complete cybersecurity protection:

- Cybersecurity consulting firms to assess and improve the company's overall security posture and provide vulnerability testing and penetration testing
- Managed security service providers (MSSPs) to monitor and manage the company's security operations 24/7
- Cybersecurity insurance providers to manage the financial risk of potential cyber incidents and data breaches
- Law firms specializing in cybersecurity to provide legal advice and guidance on data protection, privacy, and regulatory compliance
- Public relations (PR) firms to manage the company's reputation in the event of a data breach or cyber incident
- Forensic investigation firms to identify the root cause of a cyber incident and provide recommendations to prevent future attacks
- Identity and access management (IAM) providers to secure the company's authentication and authorization processes

- Security awareness training providers to educate employees on cybersecurity best practices and reduce the risk of human error

Note that the specific vendor types a company needs may vary depending on the company's size, industry, and risk profile. It is recommended that the company's cybersecurity team, with the board's input, conduct a thorough risk assessment to identify its specific cybersecurity needs and then engage the appropriate vendors.

Appendix E

Cybersecurity Resources

B oard members can utilize several key resources to improve their knowledge and awareness of cybersecurity. Some of these resources include the following:

- *Industry associations*: Many industry associations offer resources and training programs related to cybersecurity. For example, the National Association of Corporate Directors (NACD) offers cybersecurity resources and training programs for board members.
- *Government agencies*: Government agencies such as the Federal Trade Commission (FTC) and the National Institute of Standards and Technology (NIST) offer resources and guidance on cybersecurity best practices.
- *Cybersecurity consultants*: Board members can work with cybersecurity consultants to gain a better understanding of their organization's cybersecurity posture and identify areas for improvement.
- *Cybersecurity conferences and events*: Attending cybersecurity conferences and events can provide board members with the opportunity to learn about the latest cybersecurity trends and best practices.

- *Cybersecurity news sources*: Regularly reading cybersecurity news from sources such as the Cybersecurity and Infrastructure Security Agency (CISA), Information Security Media Group (ISMG), and *Security* magazine can help board members stay up to date on the latest cybersecurity threats and trends.

- *Internal resources*: Board members can also seek out resources within their own organization, such as the chief information security officer (CISO) or IT department, to better understand their organization's cybersecurity strategy and risk posture.

Appendix F

Cybersecurity Books

M any books can help board members improve their cybersecurity knowledge. Here are a few recommendations:

- *Cybersecurity for Executives: A Practical Guide*, by Gregory J. Touhill and C. Joseph Touhill: This book is specifically geared toward executives and board members and provides practical guidance on how to approach cybersecurity governance.
- *The Cybersecurity Dilemma: Hacking, Trust and Fear Between Nations,* by Ben Buchanan: This book provides an overview of the cybersecurity landscape and the impact of cyberattacks on international relations.
- *The Fifth Domain: Defending Our Country, Our Companies, and Ourselves in the Age of Cyber Threats,* by Richard A. Clarke and Robert K. Knake: This book provides an overview of the cybersecurity landscape and the role of government and private sector organizations in defending against cyber threats.
- *Click Here to Kill Everybody: Security and Survival in a Hyper-connected World,* by Bruce Schneier: This book

explores the security challenges of our hyper-connected world and provides insights into how to address them.

- *The Art of Invisibility: The World's Most Famous Hacker Teaches You How to Be Safe in the Age of Big Brother and Big Data,* by Kevin Mitnick: This book provides practical advice on protecting personal information in the digital age.

These are just a few examples; many other books are available that can provide valuable insights into cybersecurity for board members.

Appendix G

Cybersecurity Podcasts

Board members can listen to several informative and engaging cybersecurity podcasts. Here are a few suggestions:

- *Security Now!*: Hosted by Steve Gibson and Leo Laporte, this podcast covers the latest news and developments in cybersecurity.
- *The CyberWire*: Hosted by Dave Bittner, this podcast provides a daily rundown of the top cybersecurity news stories from around the world, with in-depth interviews with experts and analysis of the latest trends.
- *Darknet Diaries*: Hosted by Jack Rhysider, this podcast tells true stories of hackers, data breaches, and cyber-crime in a narrative format that is both entertaining and informative.
- *The Privacy, Security, & OSINT Show*: Hosted by Michael Bazzell, this podcast covers various topics related to online privacy, security, and open source intelligence.
- *Risky Business*: Hosted by Patrick Gray, this podcast features interviews with industry experts and thought leaders on cybersecurity, information security, and cybercrime.

- *The Redefining Cybersecurity*: Hosted by Franklin N. Miller and Sean R. Martin, this podcast covers various cybersecurity topics, including emerging threats, best practices, and risk management strategies.

These podcasts are a great way for board members to stay up to date on the latest trends and best practices in cybersecurity and gain a deeper understanding of the challenges and opportunities associated with managing cyber risk.

Appendix H

Cybersecurity Websites and Blogs

Here are some websites that board members can follow to improve their overall cybersecurity knowledge:

- *The National Institute of Standards and Technology (NIST) Cybersecurity Framework*: This is a comprehensive framework for improving cybersecurity in organizations, guiding how to identify, protect, detect, respond to, and recover from cybersecurity incidents.
- *Cybersecurity and Infrastructure Security Agency (CISA)*: This is a government agency focused on protecting the nation's critical infrastructure from physical and cyber threats.
- *Information Systems Security Association (ISSA)*: This nonprofit organization provides education, networking, and resources for cybersecurity professionals.
- *International Association of Privacy Professionals (IAPP)*: This nonprofit organization provides education, certification, and networking opportunities for privacy professionals.
- *Dark Reading*: This is a cybersecurity news and analysis website.

- *Krebs on Security*: This is a cybersecurity blog that covers the latest news and trends in the industry by Brian Krebs.
- *Schneier on Security*: This is a blog written by cybersecurity expert Bruce Schneier, providing analysis and commentary on the latest security threats and trends.
- *The Security Ledger*: This is a cybersecurity news and analysis website focusing on the Internet of Things and other emerging technologies.
- *SANS Institute*: This is a provider of cybersecurity training and certification, offering courses and resources for professionals at all levels.

Appendix I

Tabletop Exercise: Cybersecurity Incident Response

Participants:
- Board members
- Executive leadership team
- IT department representatives
- Legal department representatives
- Public relations department representatives

Exercise Overview:
This exercise tests the organization's ability to respond to a cybersecurity incident. The scenario will involve a ransomware attack on the organization's computer systems, resulting in the encryption of critical data and a demand for payment in exchange for the decryption key.

Scenario:
On a Monday morning, the organization's finance department employees notice that they cannot access critical

financial data stored on their computer systems. The affected employees report the issue to the IT department and discover that the organization's systems have been infected with ransomware. The ransomware has encrypted critical data, including financial records and customer data, and the attackers demand payment in exchange for the decryption key.

Objectives:
- Test the organization's incident response plan.
- Identify areas of weakness in the plan.
- Improve the organization's response capabilities.

Exercise Script:
1. Introduction:
   - Facilitator introduces the scenario and objectives of the exercise.
   - Participants are reminded that this is a tabletop exercise and that they should treat it as if it were an actual incident.
2. Scenario Overview:
   - Facilitator provides an overview of the scenario and the scope of the incident.
   - Participants are given time to review the information and ask any clarifying questions.
3. Incident Response Plan:
   - IT department representatives present the organization's incident response plan.
   - The plan is reviewed and discussed by the participants.
   - Areas of weakness or improvement are identified.
4. Communication:
   - Public relations department representatives discuss the communication plan for the incident.
   - Participants are given a chance to provide feedback and identify any areas of concern.

5. Legal Considerations:
   - Legal department representatives discuss legal considerations related to the incident, such as data breach notification requirements and payment of the ransom.
   - Participants discuss and identify any legal issues that need to be addressed.
6. Decision-making:
   - Participants discuss the decision-making process and who will be responsible for making key decisions during the incident.
   - A chain of command is established and documented.
7. Post-Incident Review:
   - Participants discuss the post-incident review process and identify any metrics or key performance indicators that will be used to evaluate the effectiveness of the response.
8. Conclusion:
   - Facilitator summarizes the exercise and key takeaways.
   - Participants are encouraged to provide feedback and identify areas for improvement.

Note: This is an example of a tabletop exercise script that can be modified to fit an organization's specific needs.

Appendix J

Articles

Here are a few recent news stories related to board members and cybersecurity:

- "Boards Are Having the Wrong Conversations About Cybersecurity," *Harvard Business Review* (May 2023): This article argues that boards need to discuss their organization's cybersecurity-induced risks and evaluate plans to manage those risks, rather than just relying on compliance checklists or technical jargon.
- "Are Company Boards Prepared to Deal with Cybersecurity?" *The Wall Street Journal* (June 2023): The increasing sophistication of cyberattacks and imminent SEC regulations emphasizing cyber-risk management have underscored the critical role of boards of directors in cybersecurity oversight, but a survey indicates disparities in preparedness across different companies, with factors such as company size, industry, and the presence of board members with cyber expertise significantly influencing the effectiveness of cyber-risk management.
- "Board Members Need to Look at Cybersecurity as More Than Just Protection," *Forbes* (August 2022): This article

suggests that board members need to be informed about their company's cybersecurity efforts, and consider the broader relationship between security, brand value, and business growth.

- "How Boards Can Lead Cybersecurity," *McKinsey* (February 2021): This article discusses how boards of directors should help their organizations ensure they are prepared for potential cyberattacks and what questions they should ask their IT security experts.

- "Cybersecurity Experts Have Become Targets for Board Seats," CNBC (July 2023): This article reports on the growing trend of cybersecurity experts being recruited to serve on corporate boards. The article cites a number of reasons for this trend, including the increasing importance of cybersecurity to businesses, the need for boards to have more expertise in this area, and the fact that many cybersecurity experts have the skills and experience necessary to serve on boards.

- "Why Corporate Boards Need More Cybersecurity Expertise," *The Wall Street Journal* (June 2023): This article argues that corporate boards need more cybersecurity expertise in order to effectively manage the risks posed by cyberattacks. The article cites a number of data breaches that have occurred in recent years, and argues that these breaches could have been prevented if boards had had more expertise in cybersecurity.

- "Boards of Directors Must Take Cybersecurity Seriously," *Forbes* (March 2023): This article warns that boards of directors that do not take cybersecurity seriously are putting their organizations at risk. The article cites a number of statistics that show the increasing frequency and severity of cyberattacks, and argues that boards need to take steps to protect their organizations from these attacks.

- "The Importance of Cybersecurity for Board Members," *The New York Times* (February 2023): This article discusses the importance of cybersecurity for board members. The article explains the different types of cyberattacks that organizations can face and outlines the steps that board members can take to protect their organizations from these attacks.
- "Is Your Board Prepared for New Cybersecurity Regulations?" *Harvard Business Review* (November 2022): This article highlights the increasing importance of boards' participation in cybersecurity oversight, as new regulations demand greater accountability. It emphasizes the need for boards to focus not only on cyber protection but also on cyber resilience, including recovery and business continuation plans. The article suggests that boards should develop a common language for discussing cyber risk, keep cyber resiliency on their agenda, and establish stronger relationships with cybersecurity executives to meet regulatory requirements and enhance organizational resiliency.

About the Author

Bart R. McDonough is the CEO and founder of Agio, a hybrid-managed IT and cybersecurity services provider. With more than 20 years of experience in the industry, Bart is a prominent thought leader in cybersecurity. Bart has an undergraduate degree from the University of Connecticut and a master's in business administration from Yale University.

In addition to his work with Agio, Bart is an active member of several industry associations and organizations, including the Financial Services Information Sharing and Analysis Center (FS-ISAC). His personal blog, bartmcd.com, offers insights and analysis on various cybersecurity-related topics. His writing is informed by his extensive experience in the industry and his deep commitment to helping others protect their organizations and personal information.

As a cybersecurity advisor to some of the world's largest money managers, Bart has seen firsthand how many boards are unprepared and uncertain about cybersecurity. This realization drove him to write *Cyber Guardians*, a practical guide to help board members understand the significance of cybersecurity in their respective organizations. The book is designed to equip board members with the tools and knowledge to make informed decisions and effectively manage their organization's cybersecurity risks. Through his extensive experience in the industry, Bart brings a unique perspective that will benefit not only board members but also the organizations they serve.

In *Cyber Guardians*, Bart shares his expertise and practical approach to cybersecurity with board members, helping them understand the importance of cybersecurity and providing them with actionable advice to improve their organization's cybersecurity posture. Bart's passion for educating others about cybersecurity and his commitment to helping organizations develop and maintain effective security programs shine through in every chapter of the book. With *Cyber Guardians*, board members can gain the knowledge and skills they need to become more effective cybersecurity leaders within their organizations.

Acknowledgments

To Gina Peterson—thank you for all your incredible support in my life. I will never be able to truly appreciate you for all you've done for me—personally and professionally—so let this be one more (inadequate) attempt to show my appreciation for you. Oh, and I'm sorry for all the coffee.

To Poppy, my father—thank you for adopting me and trying to stabilize our life. Thank you for loving and adoring my mother. I will forever be grateful for your care and love.

To Cheryl, Ava, and Kya—keep making the world a better and more interesting place. You are loved.

To the entire team at Agio, who have to deal with my peculiarities, intensity, and never-ending demands—I appreciate your patience, hard work, and insight. You make me better every day. #BeBetter

To my amazing group of friends—thank you for loving me, telling me when and how I could be better, making me laugh, and always being there for me and each other. Boomer (Boomer).

To John David Crooch, my fellow CEO who understands the "arena," thoughtfully checks on all his friends, and generously reviews and gives thoughtful notes and commentary—IFKYK. And a huge thank-you to Sarah, Valerie, Clifton, and Daphne for the love and the laughs. Oh, and on CyberSmart—my bad! #Bulldogs

To Troy, Marlene, and Eva—thank you for giving me a wonderful life blueprint.

To Neil—thank you for your candid honesty. You make me better. Keep creating.

To Travis and Tiffany—thank you for your endless supply of compassion. And thank you to Teagan and Tate for including me in your family fun.

To Chris and Steph—thank you for your friendship and for giving me so much peace and reassurance. Kailey and Riley, keep making the world an interesting place.

To Coach Fritts—keep coaching 'em up. Your captain. Ava and Anna—keeping being like your father.

To Johnny and Liz—pay forward what your amazing parents have given you. Frankie is lucky.

To Ryan and Michelle—thank you for a lifelong friendship. Sydney and Londyn—keep your parents on their toes.

To Kevin—well, I think we are friends.

To Jim Minatel at Wiley—you are a great collaborator and partner, and I appreciate the opportunity to again work with you and the team at Wiley.

Index